COASTAL WALKS:
NORMANDY
AND
BRITTANY

Titles in the Footpaths of Europe Series

Normandy and the Seine
Walking through Brittany
Walks in Provence
Coastal Walks: Normandy and Brittany
Walking the Pyrenees
Walks in the Auvergne

COASTAL WALKS: NORMANDY AND BRITTANY

Translated by Jane Chalk

Translation co-ordinator: Ros Schwartz

Robertson McCarta

The publishers thank the following people for their help with this book: Isabelle
Daguin, Philippe Lambert, Vicky Hayward, Gianna Rossi, Eileen Cadman

First published in 1989 by

Robertson McCarta Limited
122 King's Cross Road,
London WC1X 9DS

in association with

Fédération Française de Randonnée Pédestre
8 Avenue Marceau
75008 Paris

© Robertson McCarta Limited
© Fédération Française de Randonnée Pédestre
© Maps, Institut Geographique National (French Official Survey)
    and Robertson McCarta Limited.

Managing Editor Jackie Jones
Designed by Prue Bucknall
Production by Grahame Griffiths
Typeset by Columns of Reading
Planning Map by Robertson Merlin

Printed and bound in Hong Kong

British Library Cataloguing in Publication Data

Coastal Walks: Brittany and Normandy — (Footpaths of Europe)
    1. France. Normandy, Visitor's guides
    I. Series
    914–4'204838

    ISBN 1—85365—145—1

CONTENTS

A note from the publisher   7
Key   8
The footpaths of France, introduction by Robin Neillands   9
The Normandy–Brittany coast, introduction by John Lloyd   15

The walks and maps

Walk 1   19

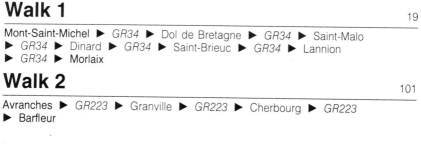

Mont-Saint-Michel ▶ *GR34* ▶ Dol de Bretagne ▶ *GR34* ▶ Saint-Malo
▶ *GR34* ▶ Dinard ▶ *GR34* ▶ Saint-Brieuc ▶ *GR34* ▶ Lannion
▶ *GR34* ▶ Morlaix

Walk 2   101

Avranches ▶ *GR223* ▶ Granville ▶ *GR223* ▶ Cherbourg ▶ *GR223*
▶ Barfleur

Index (including accommodation addresses and transport)   **148**

A note from the publisher

The books in this French Walking Guide series are published in association and with the help of the Fédération Française de la Randonnée Pédestre (French ramblers' association) — generally known as the FFRP.

The FFRP is a federal organisation and is made up of regional, local and many other associations and bodies that form its constituent parts. Individual membership is through these various local organisations. The FFRP therefore acts as an umbrella organisation overseeing the waymarking of footpaths, training and the publishing of the *Topo-guides*, detailed guides to the Grande Randonnée footpaths.

There are at present about 170 Topoguides in print, compiled and written by local members of the FFRP, who are responsible for waymarking the walks — so they are well researched and accurate.

We have translated the main itinerary descriptions, amalgamating and adapting several *Topo-guides* to create new regional guides. We have retained the basic *Topo-guide* structure, indicating length and times of walks, and the Institut Géographique National (official French survey) maps overlaid with the routes.

The information contained in this guide is the latest available at the time of going to print. However, as publishers we are aware that this kind of information is continually changing and we are anxious to enhance and improve the guides as much as possible. We encourage you to send us suggestions, criticisms and those little bits of information you may wish to share with your fellow walkers. Our address is: Robertson-McCarta, 122 King's Cross Road, London WC1X 9DS.

We shall be happy to offer a free copy of any one of these books to any reader whose suggestions are subsequently incorporated into a new edition.

It is possible to create a variety of routes by referring to the walks above and to the planning map (inside the front cover). Transport and accommodation are listed in the alphabetical index at the back of the book.

KEY

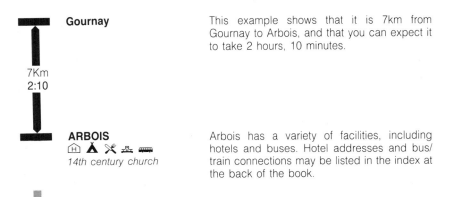

Gournay

This example shows that it is 7km from Gournay to Arbois, and that you can expect it to take 2 hours, 10 minutes.

7Km
2:10

ARBOIS
🏠 ⛺ ✕ ⛟ 🚌
14th century church

Arbois has a variety of facilities, including hotels and buses. Hotel addresses and bus/train connections may be listed in the index at the back of the book.

a grey arrow indicates an alternative route that leaves and returns to the main route.

Detour

indicates a short detour off the route to a town with facilities or to an interesting sight.

Symbols:

🏠 hotel;
⌂ youth hostel, hut or refuge;
⛺ camping;
✕ restaurant;
🍸 cafe;

⛟ shops;
🚃 railway station;
🚌 buses;
⛴ ferry;
🛈 tourist information.

THE FOOTPATHS OF FRANCE

by Robin Neillands

Why should you go walking in France? Well, walking is fun and as for France, Danton summed up the attractions of that country with one telling phrase: 'Every man has two countries,' he said, 'his own . . . and France.' That is certainly true in my case and I therefore consider it both a pleasure and an honour to write this general introduction to these footpath guides to France. A pleasure because walking in or through France is my favourite pastime, an honour because these excellent English language guides follow in the course set by those Topo-guides published in French by the Fédération Française pour la Randonnée Pédestre, which set a benchmark for quality that all footpath guides might follow. Besides, I believe that good things should be shared and walking in France is one of the most pleasant activities I know.

I have been walking in France for over thirty years. I began by rambling — or rather ambling — through the foothills of the Pyrenees, crossing over into Spain past the old Hospice de France, coming back over the Somport Pass in a howling blizzard, which may account for the fact that I totally missed two sets of frontier guards on both occasions. Since then I have walked in many parts of France and even from one end of it to the other, from the Channel to the Camargue, and I hope to go on walking there for many years to come.

The attractions of France are legion, but there is no finer way to see and enjoy them than on foot. France has two coasts, at least three mountain ranges — the Alps, Pyrenees and the Massif Central — an agreeable climate, a great sense of space, good food, fine wines and, believe it or not, a friendly and hospitable people. If you don't believe me, go there on foot and see for yourself. Walking in France will appeal to every kind of walker, from the day rambler to the backpacker, because above all, and in the nicest possible way, the walking in France is well organized, but those Francophiles who already know France well, will find it even more pleasureable if they explore their favourite country on foot.

The GR system
The Grande Randonnée (GR) footpath network now consists of more than 40,000 kilometres (25,000 miles) of long-distance footpath, stretching into every part of France, forming a great sweep around Paris, probing deeply into the Alps, the Pyrenees, and the volcanic cones of the Massif Central. This network, the finest system of footpaths in Europe, is the creation of that marvellously named organization, *la Fédération Française de Randonnée Pédestre, Comité National des Sentiers de Grande Randonnée*, which I shall abbreviate to FFRP-CNSGR. Founded in 1948, and declaring that, '*un jour de marche, huit jours de santé*,' the FFRP-CNSGR has flourished for four decades and put up the now familiar red-and-white waymarks in every corner of the country. Some of these footpaths are classic walks, like the famous GR65, *Le Chemin de St Jacques*, the ancient Pilgrim Road to Compostela, the TMB, the *Tour du Mont Blanc*, which circles the mountain through France, Switzerland and Italy, or the 600-mile long GR3, the *Sentier de la Loire*, which runs from the Ardèche to the Atlantic, to give three examples from the hundred or so GR trails available. In addition there is an abundance of GR du Pays or regional footpaths, like the *Sentier de la Haute Auvergne*,

and the *Sentier Tour des Monts d'Aubrac*. A 'Tour' incidentally, is usually a circular walk. Many of these regional or provincial GR trails are charted and waymarked in red-and-yellow by local outdoor organisations such as ABRI (Association Bretonne des Relais et Itineraires) for Brittany, or CHAMINA for the Massif Central. The walker in France will soon become familiar with all these footpath networks, national, regional or local, and find them the perfect way into the heart and heartland of France. As a little bonus, the GR networks are expanding all the time, with the detours — or *varientes* — off the main route eventually linking with other GR paths or *varientes* and becoming GR trails in their own right.

Walkers will find the GR trails generally well marked and easy to follow, and they have two advantages over the footpaths commonly encountered in the UK. First, since they are laid out by local people, they are based on intricate local knowledge of the local sights. If there is a fine view, a mighty castle or a pretty village on your footpath route, your footpath through France will surely lead you to it. Secondly, all French footpaths are usually well provided with a wide range of comfortable country accommodation, and you will discover that the local people, even the farmers, are well used to walkers and greet them with a smile, a '*Bonjour*' and a '*bon route*'.

Terrain and Climate
As a glance at these guides or any Topo-guide will indicate, France has a great variety of terrain. France is twice the size of the UK and many natural features are also on a larger scale. There are three main ranges of mountains, the Alps contain the highest mountain in Europe, the Pyrenees go up to 10,000 ft, the Massif Central peaks to over 6000 ft, and there are many similar ranges with hills which overtop our highest British peak, Ben Nevis. On the other hand, the Auvergne and the Jura have marvellous open ridge walking, the Cévennes are steep and rugged, the Ardeche and parts of Provence are hot and wild, the Île de France, Normandy, Brittany and much of Western France is green and pleasant, not given to extremes. There is walking in France for every kind of walker, but given such a choice the wise walker will consider the complications of terrain and weather before setting out, and go suitably equipped.

France enjoys three types of climate: continental, oceanic and mediterranean. South of the Loire it will certainly be hot to very hot from mid-April to late September. Snow can fall on the mountains above 4000 ft from mid-October and last until May, or even lie year-round on the tops and in couloirs; in the high hills an ice-axe is never a frill. I have used one by the Brêche de Roland in the Pyrenees in mid-June.

Wise walkers should study weather maps and forecasts carefully in the week before they leave for France, but can generally expect good weather from May to October, and a wide variety of weather — the severity depending on the terrain — from mid-October to the late Spring.

Accommodation
The walker in France can choose from a wide variety of accommodation with the assurance that the walker will always be welcome. This can range from country hotels to wild mountain pitches, but to stay in comfort, many walkers will travel light and overnight in the comfortable hotels of the *Logis de France* network.

Logis de France: The *Logis de France* is a nationwide network of small, family-run country hotels, offering comfortable accommodation and excellent food. *Logis* hotels are graded and can vary from a simple, one-star establishment, with showers and linoleum, to a four- or five-star *logis* with gastronomic menus and deep-pile carpets. All offer excellent value for money, and since there are over 5000 scattered across the French countryside, they provide a good focus for a walking day. An annual guide to the *Logis* is available from the French Government Tourist Office, 178 Piccadilly, London W1V 0AL, Tel. (01) 491 7622.

Gites d'Etape: A *gîte d'étape* is best imagined as an unmanned youth hostel for outdoor folk of all ages. They lie all along the footpath networks and are usually signposted or listed in the guides. They can be very comfortable, with bunk beds, showers, a well equipped kitchen, and in some cases they have a warden, a *guardien*, who may offer meals. *Gîtes d'étape* are designed exclusively for walkers, climbers, cyclists, cross country skiers or horse-riders. A typical price (1989) would be Fr.25 for one night. *Gîtes d'étape* should not be confused with a *Gîte de France*. A *gîte* — usually signposted as '*Gîte de France*' — is a country cottage available for a holidayt let, though here too, the owner may be more than willing to rent it out as overnight accommodation.

Youth hostels: Curiously enough, there are very few Youth Hostels in France outside the main towns. A full list of the 200 or so available can be obtained from the Youth Hostel Association (YHA), Trevelyan House, St Albans, Herts AL1 2DY.

Pensions or cafes: In the absence of an hotel, a *gîte d'étape* or a youth hostel, all is not lost. France has plenty of accommodation and an enquiry at the village cafe or bar will usually produce a room. The cafe/hotel may have rooms or suggest a nearby pension or a *chambre d'hôte*. Prices start at around Fr.50 for a room, rising to, say, Fr.120. (1989 estimate).

Chambres d'hôte: A *chambre d'hôte* is a guest room or, in English terms, a bed-and-breakfast, usually in a private house. Prices range up from about Fr.60 a night. *Chambres d'hôte* signs are now proliferating in the small villages of France and especially if you can speak a little French are an excellent way to meet the local people. Prices (1989) are from, say, Fr.70 a night for a room, not per person.

Abris: Abris, shelters or mountain huts can be found in the mountain regions, where they are often run by the *Club Alpin Francais*, an association for climbers. They range from the comfortable to the primitive, are often crowded and are sometimes reserved for members. Details from the Club Alpin Francais, 7 Rue la Boétie, Paris 75008, France.

Camping: French camp sites are graded from one to five star, but are generally very good at every level, although the facilities naturally vary from one cold tap to shops, bars and heated pools. Walkers should not be deterred by a '*Complet*' (Full) sign on the gate or office window: a walker's small tent will usually fit in somewhere. *Camping à la ferme*, or farm camping, is increasingly popular, more primitive — or less regimented — than the official sites, but widely available and perfectly adequate. Wild camping is officially not permitted in National Parks, but unofficially if you are over 1500m away from a road, one hour's walk from a *gîte* or campsite, and where possible ask permission, you should have no trouble. French country people will always assist the walker to find a pitch.

The law for walkers
The country people of France seem a good deal less concerned about their 'rights' than the average English farmer or landowner. I have never been ordered off land in France or greeted with anything other than friendliness . . . maybe I've been lucky. As a rule, walkers in France are free to roam over all open paths and tracks. No decent

walker will leave gates open, trample crops or break down walls, and taking fruit from gardens or orchards is simply stealing. In some parts of France there are local laws about taking chestnuts, mushrooms (and snails), because these are cash crops. Signs like *Réserve de Chasse*, or *Chasse Privé* indicate that the shooting is reserved for the landowner. As a general rule, behave sensibly and you will be tolerated everywhere, even on private land.

The country code
Walkers in France should obey the *Code du Randonneur*:

- Love and respect Nature.
- Avoid unnecessary noise.
- Destroy nothing.
- Do not leave litter.
- Do not pick flowers or plants.
- Do not disturb wildlife.
- Re-close all gates.
- Protect and preserve the habitat.
- No smoking or fires in the forests. (This rule is essential and is actively enforced by foresters and police.
- Stay on the footpath.
- Respect and understand the country way of life and the country people.
- Think of others as you think of yourself.

Transport
Transportation to and within France is generally excellent. There are no less than nine Channel ports: Dunkirk, Calais, Boulogne, Dieppe, Le Havre, Caen/Ouistreham, Cherbourg, Saint-Malo and Roscoff, and a surprising number of airports served by direct flights from the UK. Although some of the services are seasonal, it is often possible to fly direct to Toulouse, Poitiers, Nantes, Perpignan, Montpellier, indeed to many provincial cities, as well as to Paris and such obvious destinations as Lyon and Nice. Within France the national railway, the SNCF, still retains a nationwide network. Information, tickets and a map can be obtained from the SNCF. France also has a good country bus service and the *gare routière* is often placed just beside the railway station. Be aware though, that many French bus services only operate within the *département*, and they do not generally operate from one provincial city to the next. I cannot encourage people to hitch-hike, which is both illegal and risky, but walkers might consider a taxi for their luggage. Almost every French village has a taxi driver who will happily transport your rucksacks to the next night-stop, fifteen to twenty miles away, for Fr.50 a head or even less.

Money
Walking in France is cheap, but banks are not common in the smaller villages, so carry a certain amount of French money and the rest in traveller's cheques or Eurocheques, which are accepted everywhere.

Clothing and equipment
The amount of clothing and equipment you will need depends on the terrain, the length of the walk, the time of your visit, the accommodation used. Outside the mountain areas it is not necessary to take the full range of camping or backpacking gear. I once walked across France from the Channel to the Camargue along the Grande Randonnée footpaths in March, April and early May and never needed to use any of

the camping gear I carried in my rucksack because I found hotels everywhere, even in quite small villages.

Essential items are:
In summer: light boots, a hat, shorts, suncream, lip salve, mosquito repellent, sunglasses, a sweater, a windproof cagoule, a small first-aid kit, a walking stick.
In winter: a change of clothing, stormproof outer garments, gaiters, hat, lip salve, a companion.
In the mountains at any time: large-scale maps (1:25,000), a compass, an ice-axe. In winter, add a companion and ten-point crampons.
At any time: a phrase book, suitable maps, a dictionary, a sense of humour.

The best guide to what to take lies in the likely weather and the terrain. France tends to be informal, so there is no need to carry a jacket or something smart for the evenings. I swear by Rohan clothing, which is light, smart and functional. The three things I would never go without are light, well-broken-in boots and several pairs of loop-stitched socks, and my walking stick.

Health hazards
Health hazards are few. France can be hot in summer, so take a full water-bottle and refill it at every opportunity. A small first-aid kit is sensible, with plasters and 'mole-skin' for blisters, but since prevention is better than cure, loop-stitched socks and flexible boots are better. Any French chemist — a *pharmacie* — is obliged to render first-aid treatment for a small fee. These pharmacies can be found in most villages and large towns and are marked by a green cross.

Dogs are both a nuisance and a hazard. All walkers in France should carry a walking stick to fend off aggressive curs. Rabies — *la rage* — is endemic and anyone bitten must seek immediate medical advice. France also possesses two types of viper, which are common in the hill areas of the south. In fairness, although I found my walking stick indispensable, I must add that in thirty years I have never even seen a snake or a rabid dog. In case of real difficulty, dial 17 for the police and the ambulance.

Food and wine
One of the great advantages with walking in France is that you can end the day with a good meal and not gain an ounce. French country cooking is generally excellent and good value for money, with the price of a four-course menu starting at about Fr.45. The ingredients for the mid-day picnic can be purchased from the village shops and these also sell wine. Camping-Gaz cylinders and cartridges are widely available, as is 2-star petrol for stoves. Avoid naked fires.

Preparation
The secret of a good walk lies in making adequate preparations before you set out. It pays to be fit enough to do the daily distance at the start. Much of the necessary information is contained in this guide, but if you need more, look in guidebooks or outdoor magazines, or ask friends.

The French
I cannot close this introduction without saying a few words about the French, not least because the walker in France is going to meet rather more French people than, say, a motorist will, and may even meet French people who have never met a foreigner before. It does help if the visitor speaks a little French, even if only enough to say 'bonjour' and 'Merci' and 'S'il vous plait'. The French tend to be formal and it pays to be

polite, to say 'hello', to shake hands. I am well aware that relations between France and England have not always been cordial over the last six hundred years or so, but I have never met with hostility of any kind in thirty years of walking through France. Indeed, I have always found that if the visitor is prepared to meet the French halfway, they will come more than halfway to greet him or her in return, and are both friendly and hospitable to the passing stranger.

As a final tip, try smiling. Even in France, or especially in France, a smile and a 'pouvez vous m'aider?' (Can you help me?) will work wonders. That's my last bit of advice, and all I need do now is wish you 'Bonne Route' and good walking in France.

THE NORMANDY–BRITTANY COAST

by John Lloyd

The coast of northern Brittany and Normandy offers some wonderful walking experiences for Britiah walkers looking for a change of view. The scenery is enormously varied, with a mixture of seascapes and landscapes, while here and there smart holiday resorts, picturesque fishing villages and tiny hamlets add even more interest and a chance of a break. At the same time walking this coast isn't a great test of stamina, for while there are undulations, they are rarely severe.

But perhaps the greatest advantage of walking in this part of France is that it is just a ferry trip away. Cross over to Cherbourg, Saint-Malo or Roscoff by ferry and you can descend the gangplank in your walking boots and immediately step out on a GR footpath.

Both the routes described here start (or finish) at the distinctive monastery island of Mont St. Michel, one of the best known sights in France. It lies at the mouth of the Couesnon, the natural boundary between Brittany and Normandy, and from its walls you can walk west along the GR34 towards Morlaix or east along the GR22 and GR223 towards Barfleur on the north-eastern tip of the Cotentin Peninsula. That's a total distance of 850 kilometres or so, much of which was originally trodden by customs men on the lookout for smugglers.

Obviously you can't expect to walk all of that in one go, not unless you've got a few weeks to spare, but with those three ferry crossings to choose from and good rail and reasonable bus connections in France, it's fairly easy to plan a much shorter section for yourself. Good sections for a weekend or more are from Cherbourg to Barfleur and returning via a loop to St. Vaast-la-Hougue, or from Saint-Malo to Mont St. Michel.

If you do plan to walk the full length of either path, a good idea is to arrive at one ferry port and leave by another. For instance, for the GR34 arrive at Roscoff and leave from Saint-Malo, and for the GR22/GR223 arrive at Saint-Malo and leave from Cherbourg. Roscoff is about 28km by bus or train from the start of the GR34 at Morlaix, while the journey between Saint-Malo and Mont St. Michel involves a train ride to Pontorson and a bus to Mont St. Michel. At the end of the GR223 there's a bus service from Barfleur to Cherbourg.

Another advantage of walking through Brittany and Normandy is that you don't have to carry large quantities of food and drink with you. You're never far from a village or a town where you can buy food, and there are plenty of restaurants if you want to linger over lunch. If you're on a budget, try a sweet crêpe or savoury galette with a glass of cider at one of the many crêperies.

Seafood could play a major part in your diet in this part of the world. Norman and Breton clams and mussels are famous, and so are the mouth-watering oysters, especially those from Cancale on the GR34 and St. Vaast-la-Hougue just south of Barfleur on the GR223. Typical cheeses of the area are Camembert, Pont l'Eveque and Livarot, while a smoked sausage or two makes a tasty trail snack.

Accommodation shouldn't prove a problem, though if you can, book your room in advance, if only by phone on the morning before you arrive. On the other hand if you do leave it to chance, there's always the possibility you'll stumble across a real bargain. A twin-room for around 40 francs per person isn't unheard of, though that's the kind of luck that doesn't normally come my way. I usually discover the bargains in the morning when I don't need them. If you're planning to camp, you'll find plenty of sites near the resorts.

So what's this stretch of coastline between Morlaix and Barfleur really like? As I've said already, you'll be met with constantly changing panoramas, particularly on the Breton section as the footpath forever changes direction to take in the many inlets and coves along its length. Off-shore there are hundreds of rocky islands, some quite tiny which disappear at high tide, others much larger, crowned maybe with a chateau or a lighthouse.

Morlaix, in a steep-sided river valley and dominated by a huge railway viaduct, is a pleasant town to start or finish a walk. Buy any supplies you need here, then you can join the GR34 heading north towards the Pointe de Primel.

In the early stages the path loops inland from time to time, but near the lovely little port of Locquirec it rejoins the coast, just in time for the wonderful views along the Corniche de l'Armorique. After another brief wander the path follows the coast to Lannion, an old Breton town on the river Leguer, where every Thursday a colourful market spreads along the river bank and through the steep old streets.

Beyond Lannion the path reaches the Pink Granite Coast (Côte de Granit Rose), so called because of the extraordinary colour of the rocks, some of which have names ot test your imagination. See if you can spot Napoleon's Hat, the Elephant, the Rabbit, the Umbrella or the Corkscrew.

It's quite a well populated part of the coast, with smart resorts like Trébeurden, Trégastel-Plage, Ploumanac'h and Perros-Guirec clustered round pine-fringed bays. But then comes a lonely stretch, with deserted beaches, few people and only the occasional hamlet.

Tréguier, a picturesque little town of cobbled streets and old houses, is the next watering-hole of any size, and this is followed by more quiet coastline round to the Pointe de l'Arcouest which looks out to the largest island along this coast, the Ile de Bréhat. Beyond Paimpol, the path passes the ruins of Beauport Abbey and the resorts of St.-Quay, Etables and Binic, before turning inland to St. Brieuc, a large town where you should find any supplies you haven't been able to obtain en route.

The path soon gets back to the coast, passing through Le Val-André and Erquy, two resorts with the finest sandy beaches in northern Brittany, before climbing up to the spectacular Cap d'Erquy. Farther on, there are even more dramatic views from the high cliffs of Cap Fréhel. Round the large, angular Baie de la Frenaye, guarded by the impressive Fort la Latte, you come to St. Cast, and the start of a much frequented holiday region. St. Jacut follows St. Cast, then come lovely St. Briac, St. Lunaire and that most English of resorts, Dinard. If you've had trouble communicating with the natives so far, you won't here. English is spoken everywhere.

A short-cut, a ferry ride across the river Rance, will take you to the walled town of Saint-Malo, but by taking the footpath across the Rance barrage, you'll see far more of this interesting town. After Saint-Malo and Parame, there's more quiet coastline with secluded beaches where sunbathers are frequently bottomless as well as topless, and then the Pointe de Grouin, which offers your first glimpse of Mont St. Michel, little more than a pimple on the horizon.

South of Cancale, the scenery undergoes a marked change. The rocky coastline gives way to salt marshes and though there is an alternative path along the coast, the main route heads inland for a brief climb over Mont Dol to Dol de Bretagne. From there, the path follows a ridge of hills to Roz-sur-Couesnon, before re-crossing the polders back to the coast for the run-in to Mont St. Michel.

Across the marshes to the east of Mont St. Michel, the GR22 heads off in the direction of Avranches. This is only a short path, because at Avranches it meets the

GR223 which winds out to the coast before its long trek up the Cotentin Peninsular. Though it's now the other side of the bay, there are superb views of Mont St. Michel. The GR223 doesn't stay as close to the coast as the Breton path, but often wanders inland. At Carolles for instance, rather than take the walker through a sprawl of seaside towns at Jullouville, Kairon Plage and St. Pair, the path turns inland and doesn't return to the sea until Granville, a lively resort and yachting centre dominated by a rocky headland.

Northwards, the path follows the coast for a while, then turns inland to Brehal and wanders more or less parallel to the coast to Coutances, the religious centre for the area and noted for its magnificent cathedral. North of Coutances, the path meanders about, picking its way through a dense network of minor roads, past the château at Pirou and then across moorland, and is beyond Lessay before its turn back to the sea.

This coast is nothing like as rugged as Brittany's, though there's the occasional river estuary like those at Portbail with its unspoiled harbour and Barneville-Carteret with its bustling quaysides. Farther north the path steers away from the coast again until north of Le Rozel it rounds the cliffs of Flamanville, passes the nuclear power station under construction there and then skirts through barren countryside behind the broad Vauville Bay.

Cap de la Hague is wild and desolate and not the place to be on a wet and windy day. Beyond the headland though it should be relatively sheltered for the hike to Cherbourg.

From Cherbourg, big and ugly like most major ports, the path heads inland once more, but only as far as Maupertus airport. There it turns north to the coast and finally arrives, via the headlands at Cap Levy and the Pointe de Barfleur, at the pleasant little resort and harbour of Barfleur.

17

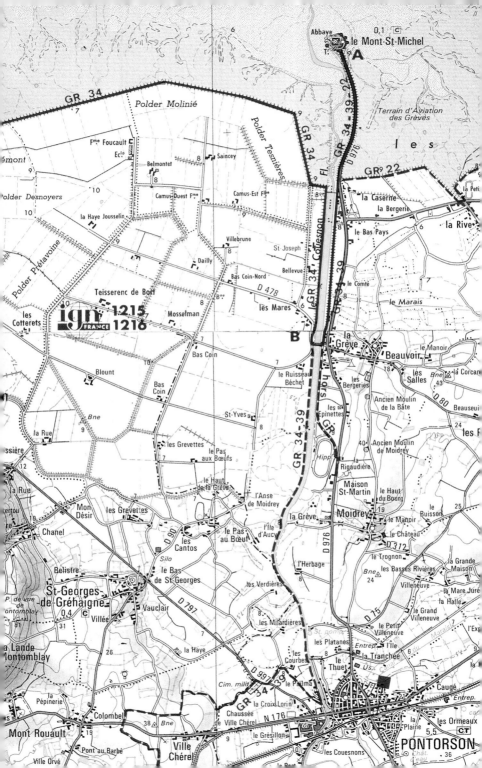

WALK 1

2Km
0:30

2Km
0:30

LE MONT-SAINT-MICHEL BAY

ⓗ Ⲁ ⛴ 🚌 🚃

This vast bay is an enchanted area, full of legends of vanished villages, and stories of the eternal struggle between the Archangel Michael and the Devil.

The area directly surrounding Le Mont-Saint-Michel is worth exploring, but only if the tide is right – it comes in very quickly and unevenly and can cut you off. There are also patches of sand which conceal deep troughs of water, indiscernible to the unpractised eye (the infamous 'shifting sands'), which would leave you floundering.

LA CASERNE

ⓗ ⌂ Ⲁ ✕ 🚃

Pont de Beauvoir
Detour *30 mins*
LE MOIDREY
⌂

The walk starts from the bay. Le Mont-Saint-Michel, called the 'Marvel of the West', is reached after a climb up granite cliffs. Go through the postern gates and walk down La Grande Rue. You can turn off the street when you get to the church to follow a quieter route. Arriving at the west gate, you can look down onto the entrance to the mount from terraced gardens. You also have a good view of the coast as it stretches inland (south) towards Pontorson. From Gabriel tower you can see westwards beyond the River Couesnon to the great grassy stretches of the polders. At the abbey entrance a magnificent staircase leads to the starting point for the guided tour (45 minutes). From the northern ramparts you can see the little island of Tombelaine and the Cotentin coastline.

As it leaves the mount, the GR follows the seawall south. This wall, built in 1897, has provoked a lot of controversy. It has caused sand to build up around the mount by preventing the sea from flowing freely round the island, and it may eventually be replaced by a bridge. If you want to avoid walking along a stretch of road, take a bus from Mont-Saint-Michel railway station to La Caserne or Beauvoir bridge.

Beware! You must not cross the River Couesnon near La Caserne over the barrier floodgate. Any walkers who do so do it at their own risk. You have to make a detour via Beauvoir bridge.
At La Caserne, therefore, the GR34 (also the GR39 at this point) heads south along the dike on the east bank of the Couesnon, to Pont de Beauvoir.

Detour see left. Continue on the east bank of the Couesnon until just after the racecourse.

Cross the bridge, and turn right (north) following the GR34 along the west bank of the Couesnon back to the barrier floodgate opposite La Caserne. (Remember: you are for-

9Km
2:15

Junction of two dikes

8Km
2

CHERRUEIX

5Km
1:15

Detour, *15 mins*
L'AUMÔNE

LE VIVIER-SUR-MER

2Km
0:30

HIREL

3Km
0:45

LES QUATRE-SALINES

bidden to cross this floodgate.) Beyond the floodgate there are no markings on the dike. Follow the dike westwards to the first cross-roads, and turn right (north). The fertile polders behind the dike were regained from the sea in the nineteenth century. The sea only comes up to the dike at very high tides. There is a large stretch of grass outside the dike, where salt-meadow sheep graze. The flat landscape is only broken by raised shepherd huts (do not go into them) and hunters' hides. It is worth exploring around the dike, but also worth returning to the dike every now and again to get a good view of Mont-Saint-Michel. There is a road on the left leading to Poulder Foulon farm 6 kilometres after the floodgate. Ignore this, and continue along the dike for 1 kilometres, where you will find the remains of a landing stage, and another dike running inland. The markings for the GR start again here.

Alternative route to Hirel and Dol. This junction is the departure point for an unmarked alternative route leading to Hirel, and makes a circular route of 45 kilometres by joining up with the GR34 again at Hirel, and passing later through Dol-de-Bretagne. This walk to Hirel runs along the coastline, sometimes following the dike, sometimes the roads. It is shown as a dotted line on the maps.

See map on page 22

See map on page 24

This is where you rejoin the GR34. At the junction of the two dikes, the GR34 leaves the sea and turns left (south) along private dikes between the polders. Lined with poplar trees, these dikes are sometimes overgrown with tall grass, or scattered with grazing cattle and sheep. Make sure that you close all gates and stick to the set path. You then take the road leading away from the polders towards the hamlet of Quatre-Salines.

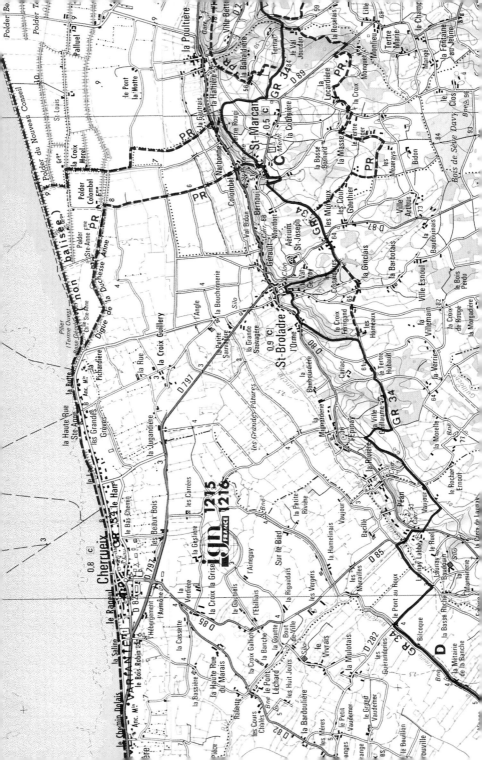

LE BAS DU PALAIS

1Km
0:15

ROZ-SUR-COUESNON

Paul Féval based his work 'La Fée des Grèves' (Fairy of the Shore) here. Bakers sell a curious flat loaf of bread, which they call 'tourteau' (cattle cake).

4Km
1

SAINT-MARCAN

Detours, *There are several short walks in the area: 1) Walk round Saint-Marcan (1 hour) – marked in white on signposts; 2) Walk around the surrounding area, through small wood on the plateau (3 hours) – signposted in yellow; 3) Walk through surrounding grasslands (3 hours 30 mins) – signposted in orange.*

3Km
1

SAINT-BROLADRE

Sculptured cross in the cemetery; old houses.

The GR cuts across the road (D797) at a cluster of houses named Le Bas du Palais. You now find yourself at the foot of a cliff; the sea used to come in as far as this point before the polders were built. Take the road leading to Roz-sur-Couesnon, and turn off at the first hairpin bend along a rather overgrown path which wends its way through the scrub up to the public gardens at Roz-sur-Couesnon. From here, you have a magnificent view out over the polders and the long straight line of poplar trees to Mont-Saint-Michel in the distance. The GR now enters the market town of Roz-sur-Couesnon.

The GR heads west out of Roz-sur-Couesnon along the road, and then drops away to the left down an overgrown track and crosses a stream. Take the sunken path back up to the road, turn left and then follow a tarmac track off to the right (west) which climbs upwards to give you a good view of the bay. Further on it cuts across two roads and runs past a campsite. You come out close to the gîte at Saint-Marcan.

The GR heads west out of Saint-Marcan. If you turn right and then left at the first crossroads, you can visit the 'Petit Mont-Saint-Michel', a model version of the 'original', which has been skilfully reconstructed by a local artist. The GR skirts a small pond, and then follows a dirt track to a road edged here and there with shale outcrops and which looks down on Saint-Broladre. Pass through the hamlet of Les Muriaux and follow the road to a pond where you turn right (north) along a small path, which will take you to the final meadow on your right. From here you have a good view over the bay and Saint-Joseph sanatorium, an elegant stone building. The GR drops down into an area of woods, ponds and waterfalls, and comes out at Saint-Broladre.

The GR runs alongside the Saint-Broladre cemetery, and then heads towards L'Orme, the outlying part of the town. Head left on the D80 for a few metres and then turn off left when you reach a bend to the right in the road, taking a path that runs between two barns. You will cross a private wood (access has kindly been granted to ramblers), cross a

23

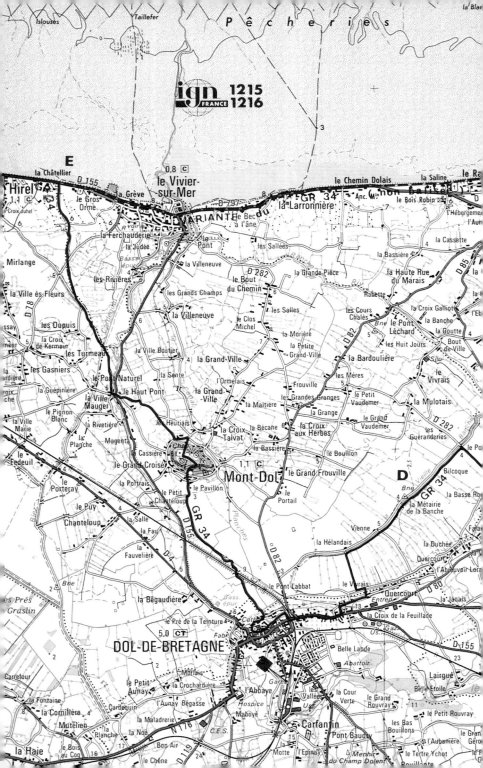

On your left, is the Les Homeaux manor house with its beautiful portal.

11Km
2:45

stream and then arrive at a road.

The GR passes through Le Tertre-Hubault, and then runs alongside the ancient manor house at La Ville-Guillaume. Little of this is left now, only the ruined chapel beside the farm is still standing. Continue westwards along a paved lane then turn right (north), along a farm track. Turn left (west) at the first crossroads along a paved road which subsequently becomes tarmacadam. From this point, you have a superb view out over the marshes and the bay. After the cluster of houses at Vaujour, drop down right to the D80. Turn right along it, then take the second turning on the left, and make for Le Pont-au-Roux, which marks the beginning of the Dol marshes. When you get to Le Pont-au-Roux, take the dirt track on your left. From here onwards the route follows a bridle path signposted in orange. You run alongside a canal, La Vieille Banche.

2 kilometres further on, you reach (but do not cross) a wooden bridge. Turn left (south), and take the path that runs alongside a field: make sure that you don't damage the crops or fences. The GR then dives down a tunnel underneath a busy road, and takes a road westwards to the outskirts of Dol. It makes for the town centre.

DOL-DE-BRETAGNE

Saint-Samson, a 13th century cathedral, well known for its size, two sculptured porches and large 14th century stained glass window. In the Middle Ages, the faithful would make a great 'Tro Breiz' (tour of Brittany) which took in all the holy places, Saint-Samson was one of these.

2Km
0:30

In Dol town, the GR turns right after the railway bridge and follows the Promenade des Douves (Dove Walk). It goes along a shopping street, and then follows a quaint tarmac street with old houses on each side to Saint-Samson cathedral.

The GR then drops down to the left (north) towards the marshes and takes a winding road to the village of Mont-Dol.

MONT-DOL

Like Mont-Saint-Michel, Mont-Dol is a small granite island surrounded by

The GR34 takes the road through the village and then takes a sharp bend up towards the top of Mont-Dol. You will pass magnificent chestnut trees on this part of the walk, and a superb view awaits you at the top. Keep

*legends of Saint Michael's
struggle with the Devil.
Today it is no more than a
headland which stands out
against the surrounding area.
Palaeolithic flints and
remains have been found
here, and a sacrificial altar
from a temple of Diana.*

La Châtellier

5Km
1:15

HIREL
4Km
1

**SAINT-BENOÎT-DES-
ONDES**
3Km
0:45

**Pointe de
Château-Richeux**

2Km
0:30

1:15

slightly left of the road, and make your way
across the grasslands, ensuring that all gates
are firmly closed. Drop down a steep path
towards the north-west, and follow a series of
small roads, some paved and some tarmac,
across the marshes and canals to the coast
and the tiny hamlet of La Châtellier on the
D155.

From La Châtellier there is an unmarked
alternative route, which leads right (east) to
Vivier-sur-Mer and Cherrueix, and rejoins the
GR34 at an intersection of several dikes just
after Chapelle de Sainte-Anne. (See dotted
line on the map.)

From La Châtellier, the GR34 takes the D155
left to Hirel.

The GR34 continues west along the coast,
following the D155 through Vildé-le-Marine and
Saint-Benoît-des-Ondes.

As you leave Saint-Benoît, you should turn left
off the D155 and follow a path north-west
which runs parallel to the road. The GR then
cuts back across the D155 and follows the
coastline again to La Pointe de Château-
Richeux.

From here onwards, the GR follows a new path
which skirts the houses and overlooks the
shore. This is the pedestrian footpath along the
coast and is signposted by a green arrow.
Further on, when you come to a property
surrounded by walls, follow the GR as it drops
down onto the beach. Shortly afterwards you
leave the shore and take the narrow passage
running between two walls. Follow a dirt track
which runs in front of Vauleraut château — this
takes you to a narrow one-way road. (The
alternative GR34a route starts here.)

Alternative route (GR34a) Terrelabouët to
Plage du Guesclin. This signposted alternative
route cuts 9 kilometres off the GR34 walk,
rejoining it at Plage du Guesclin and makes a
circular trip of 22 kilometres around Cancale.

The itinerary traces the steps of the old 'Parishioners' Walk' which was the route taken by processions from Cancale to Chapelle du Verger (Orchard Chapel). Go left past Terrelabouët on the narrow road described above, cut across the D76, and then follow a series of dirt tracks north, which run alongside fields where early vegetables are grown. Cross the D355, skirt round a valley and then plunge into a private wooded dell. Cross the D201 and you will then find yourself at Plage du Guesclin, where you meet up with the GR34.

Plage du Guesclin

2Km
0:30

The GR follows the narrow road right to La Houle, which is a small fishing port on the outskirts of Cancale.

CANCALE

Cancale is famed for its oysters, at low tide, you can see the tight latticework of the oyster beds. Also the home of the Amis des Chemins de Ronde (Friends of the Footpath Association), which is trying to rescue and restore the coastal footpaths.

8Km
2

The GR runs alongside the port until it comes to the north jetty. A monument with a plaque marks the beginning of the *chemin de ronde* (footpath) which heads off up a paved lane. It follows the footpath over undulating countryside, and you may find that the tracks are sometimes difficult to find as there are insufficient props for signposts. Make sure that you don't take one of the numerous paths which lead down to the beach by mistake. When you come to the rather gloomy Rocher de Cancale and the fortified Île de Cancale the GR skirts an estate. Be careful if you are coming from the opposite direction, as you may not notice the change of direction. The GR then crosses several small marinas until it comes to the beach at Port-Mer, where you will find restaurants and cafes. Follow the sea-front for about 100 metres and then head off again along the footpath. You will pass a campsite and then come to the start of La Pointe du Grouin in front of the houses. If you go out onto the point, return here to continue the walk.

POINTE DU GROUIN

You can walk out to the tip of the point along the small paths through the gorse. This is a wild location, especially when the sea is rough, but views of the surrounding area are superb.

The GR follows the coastline westwards, initially along paths overgrown with gorse where signposts may be infrequent, and then along a recently made track. Drop down to Plage des Saussayes and go along the shore. Cross a stream and climb up to the right beside a fence. You join the coastal footpath, which heads round La Pointe de la Moulière with its old fortress, and then runs alongside Plage du Verger (Orchard beach). Then take the road south-west to Chapelle du Verger.

5Km
1:30

From La Pointe du Grouin to Saint-Malo and Dinan, the coastal footpath is the scene of a small battle: bit by bit the authorities are acquiring the land, helped by the bye-law governing right of way beside the sea. The GR is having to adapt as these coastguard footpaths are regained for use, and you will find that there will be frequent small changes to the route.

Chapelle du Verger
The sailors of Cancale used to make pilgrimages to this ancient chapel. Votive offerings on display.

At the chapel, the GR follows the coastal footpath again to the Dôles look-out tower. You should make your way round a campsite and then drop down into the pine trees until you come to a beach. At this point, take the dirt track on your right. The GR circumnavigates the Pointe du Nid (Nest Point) along the coastal footpath. Follow the dike down to Plage du Guesclin.

Plage du Guesclin
✕

Alternative route GR34a. Plage du Guesclin to Terrelabouët (see page 27). Here you join up on your left with the GR34a alternative route (signposted) which makes a circular 22 kilometre walk round Cancale and rejoins the GR34 (past Terrelabouët) on the other side of the D76.

From here, work is in progress on the coastal footpath. It is passable, but parts are still overgrown.

Take great care on the cliff edge!

The GR34 runs along Plage du Guesclin on the sand below the dike.

Beside a small house at the western tip of Plage du Guesclin, the GR ventures onto La Pointe des Grands-Nez (Big Noses Point). If the going on the point becomes too difficult, retrace your steps and then head right alongside the field towards a thicket — this is private land, and there are few signposts.

Roz-Ven
Novelist Colette lived here and her story Le Blé en Herbe (The Ripening Seed) is based here.

At Roz-Ven (see left) you have two options: 1) at high tide, you can follow the marked route which heads south round La Touesse beach along the D201. On your left, you will see a small footpath (a 12 kilometre walk), signposted with white circles, which leads to the château of La Ville-ès-Offrans. (See dotted line on map); 2) at low tide, you can climb down

7Km
2

LA GUIMORAIS

2.5Km
0:40

Detour *3 hrs*
La Ville-es-Offrans

ROTHÉNEUF

4.5Km
1:10

across the rocks to Plage de la Touesse and head round the rocky promontory (marked with a dotted line on the map). At the far end of Plage de la Touesse, the GR takes the coastal footpath to La Pointe du Meinga. Here, you should take the path through the gorse and then leave the coast to follow a route heading due south, which is used by the farm Les Nielles. You will subsequently come to La Guimorais.

The GR takes a path on the right leading to Etang du Lupin, which is blocked off by a ruined dike. This dike may be under water, if so, cross over the dike at the other end of the lake. Make your way along the muddy coastline, which gradually becomes rocky then sandy as you approach Rothéneuf. This part of the route is difficult at high tide, as the sea covers part of the beach at Rothéneuf harbour. When the sea is in, leave the beach and turn right onto the D201.

Detour, see left. From here you can detour and visit the 17th century château of La Ville-ès-Offrans. Take the diversion which heads southwards and is signposted to the château. This continues after the château along a PR path, marked in white circles, and rejoins the GR at the south end of Plage de la Touesse. This whole circular detour is 12 kilometres long.
The GR follows either the road leading down to the beach or the D201 to Rothéneuf.

The GR turns right at the first street in Rothéneuf, and then runs alongside a field in front of an estate. It leads to the chapel at Notre-Dame-des-Flots (Our Lady of the Waves). Ramblers coming from the opposite direction (west) can, at this point, assess whether the level of the tide will enable them to proceed along Rothéneuf beach and to the Etang du Lupin. You should pass the entrance to the Rochers Sculptées (rocks sculpted by Abbé Fouré) and rejoin the beach at Plage du Val, where the route follows a bridle path. Continue along the roads and dirt tracks to La Pointe de la Varde and skirt this stretch of former military territory. The GR arrives at Le Pont at the far north-east tip of the beach.

Le Pont

5Km
1:15

SAINT-MALO

Old walled town ravaged in World War II, but reconstruction has preserved much of its character. Views of the town, the River Rance and the surrounding ports from ramparts; tomb of the French writer Châteaubriand on the little island of Le Grand-Bé, accessible at low tide.

0:10

DINARD

Boat trips in the summer to Saint-Malo.

The markings lead you along the road running parallel to the coast, but you can walk along beside the sea all the way to Saint-Malo, tide permitting (links between the road and the beach are signposted), or you can take a bus all the way to the old corsair town.

The best way to cross the Rance estuary so that you can rejoin the GR34 at Dinard, is to take the 10 minute boat trip across. This service is seasonal. You will get excellent views of the estuary, the ramparts of Saint-Malo and the old city fortress. Catch the boat at the south side of the walled town. Full details of the service at the harbour station at Saint-Malo.

Alternative route Saint-Malo to ferry station at Dinard across the Barrage de la Rance. If you want to walk across, follow the unmarked GR to the *barrage* (dam) over the Rance. (You can cut considerable time off the journey by catching a local bus at Saint-Servan to Rosais hospital.) In Saint-Malo, follow the locks and the ferry car park to Saint-Servan beach and then take the pleasant coast road to the Promenade du Fort d'Aleth. Continue past Tour Solidor, skirt the quays and then turn into a street underneath an arch. At low tide, you can turn right, across the public gardens, and go down a flight of steps onto the shore — but be careful if the tide is coming in. At high tide, you can make your way round Sainte-Croix church and follow the little streets to Rosais beach. From the beach, a pleasant coastal footpath leads to the dam, and you cross it on a footbridge. You join up with the GR34c on the other side. If you now head north, you will take about 1½ hrs to reach Dinard. You rejoin the GR34 at the ferry.

When you leave the ferry, take the GR34 north to the Promenade du Moulinet and make for La Pointe du Moulinet. Just before you get there, follow the steps down to the sea, watching out for heavy seas at high tide. Continue along Plage de l'Ecluse and the beach at Saint-

11Km
2:45

SAINT-LUNAIRE
🏠 🛖 🍴 ⚓ 🚌
Norman church.

8Km
2

SAINT-BRIAC
🏠 🛖 🍴 ⚓ 🚌

3.5Km
1

LANCIEUX
🏠 🛖 🍴 ⚓ 🚌

*The schorre, a vast area of
mud and slime covered with*

Enogat. Steps hewn out of the rockface will then take you back up the top of the cliff. Follow the coastal path and continue on past Pointe de Roche Pelée (Stripped Rock Point) to Plage de la Fourberie. The GR follows a slope up off the near end of the beach, and then heads along Rue Bergerat and turns right, along the road (D786) to Saint-Lunaire. When you reach the cluster of houses at La Tertre-Barrière just before the modern cross, turn right (north) to Le Nick. From here, take the coastal footpath through the bracken, making sure not to go all the way down to the beach. When you have got right round the headland, drop down to the shore, and when you reach the D786 again, turn right for a few metres, continuing along a long beach and heading back up to the road in Saint-Lunaire.

The GR then heads right (north) to the Pointe du Décollé, from where you can see eastwards along the coast to La Pointe de la Varde and westwards to Cap Fréhel. Follow the D264 which bends left, and then take the path on your right and climb the steps to a rocky creek. Continue along Plage de Longchamp, and then take the coastal footpath to the Pointe de la Garde-Guérin, close to a golf course (watch out for golf balls, and make sure you don't distract the players), and then on to Pointe de la Haye. When you come to a large raised car-park, head left (east) to Les Tertres, and wend your way through the streets, via La Rue des Mimosas to Béchet beach (not labelled on map).

The GR34 heads left along the sea front, and then disappears down a little street on your right to the Lancieux road (D786), where you turn right (south). The GR runs alongside the mouth of the River Frémur and then turns right over the bridge. On the other side, turn off the D786 and continue straight on along the coast road to Lancieux.

After about ½ kilometre, a road on your right will take you to Saint-Cieux beach, and you can then follow the coastal footpath all the way to the beach at Les Briantais. The GR continues along the back of Lancieux bay, at the edge of the *schorre.*

grass and other vegetation, is covered by the sea at very high tides. You are sheltered here by a dike that protects the polders.

The slikke, *unlike the* schorre, *is an area of mud that cannot support any form of vegetation because it is covered by the sea more* frequently.

16Km
4

Continue along the shore until you come to the D768, where you have two options: 1) if the tide is in and there is a lot of water in the bay, take the D768 right and then turn right along the D26 towards Saint-Jacut. A path, again on your right, will take you out to the Pointe de la Justice; 2) if it is low tide, drop down to the right immediately after the bridge over the River Drouet, and walk across the bay to La Pointe de la Justice (route not marked on map). You will have to take care, as this route means fording several small deep channels, which can be difficult to see underneath the vegetation. Sea-lavender, glasswort and obiones grow here. When you reach Pointe de la Justice, make for the beaches at La Manchette and La Pissotte and skirt round Port du Châtelet. If you continue north you will come to the harbour at La Houle-Causseul (not labelled), and a coastal footpath will lead you on to the beach at Le Rougeret. Stay on the road until you come to the tip of La Pointe du Chevet (Bedhead Point), and from here you have a view out over the Île des Hébihens. Retrace your steps until you come to the road running south to the area of land called L'Abbaye, and make your way round this. Turn right to Plage les Haas and then continue along the road to La Banche beach at Saint-Jacut-de-la-Mer.

SAINT-JACUT-DE-LA-MER

The GR runs along above La Banche beach until it comes to a raised platform beside the D62. At high tide, take this road south and then turn right along the road to Vauvet beach. The GR drops down some steps to Plage du Ruet, continues over Plage de Vauvert and then passes Les Pierres Sonnantes (the Ringing Rocks), the origins of which are unknown. Follow the dunes, cross a field and then take a path on your right down to a pile of rather imposing ruins, which is all that is left now of the château of Gilles-de-Bretagne. The GR runs along a path and onto the road to Le Guildo.

4Km
1

LE GUILDO

At Le Guildo, the GR heads right along the D786, and crosses a bridge over the River Arguenon. A little further on, you should turn right along a road which passes the château of Le Val and continue north to the beach at Quatre-Vaux. You should turn off right just

12Km
3

SAINT-CAST-LE-GUILDO

Column commemorating the battle of Saint-Cast on the beach.

13Km
3:15

PORT-À-LA-DUC

5Km
1:15

before Sainte-Brigitte along a path leading to the Bois-ès-Lucas road, and then take this road to La Ville Eon. Continue to Le Biot and then on to La Pointe du Bay, where you have a good view of the currents in Baie de L'Arguenon. A coastal footpath takes you on to Plage de Pen-Guen, and you should make your way round the shore. Follow the road to the hamlet of La Garde and then turn right towards La Pointe de la Garde. You will pass the statue of Notre-Dame-de-le-Garde, and then you can drop down some steps to Les Mielles beach at Saint-Cast-le-Guido.

When you reach the end of Les Mielles beach, take the road which drops down to Port-Jacquet and then climb up towards the signal station. You will be able to see the monument to the *Evadés de France* (escaped prisoners) as you continue along, and a coastal footpath will lead you to the beach at La Mare. Here you can see a monument to the meteorological frigate *Laplace*. The path continues above the beaches at La Pissote, La Fresnaye and La Fosse. When you reach Port-Saint-Jean, you should drop down to the beach and ford a stream, which will take you to the Moulin-de-la-Mer (sea mill) dike. Cross this and take the road to the little village of Saint-Germain, where there is a chapel and a good viewpoint. Follow the paved road south-west to the D786, and take this road right. You will pass a cluster of houses at Les Salines, where you can see the old salt marshes on your left, and you should then continue along the dike. When you reach the outpost of Le Fournel, turn right off the road and then right again until you find the coastal footpath: the GR continues on this round La Pointe de Crissouët. Drop down to the back of the bay and take the path, which may well be flooded, to Port-à-la-Duc.

The GR takes the D786 over the Frémur bridge and then heads right in a north-easterly direction along the road to Port-Nieux. At low tide, you can actually go along beside the sea by taking a route over the *schorre* (see p. 37) to Port-Nieux. The GR follows the road to Grand-Trécelin, and then takes a path and another road to the D16A. This is a busy road, but for the moment, you have to follow it for 1.5 kilometres to the cluster of houses at La Motte.

41

La Motte
Detour, *15 mins*
LA VILLE-HARDRIEUX
⌂

*As you make your way along
this path, you have
magnificent views out over
the sea. You will find
yourself surrounded by lush
vegetation, with several
mediterranean species
which are peculiar to this
Forte la Latte area.*

4Km
1

Just before La Motte, the GR heads off right along a lane and then takes an almost hidden path down to Port-Saint-Géran. Climb up the approach road and then turn right. You should continue on over several crossroads and then follow the coastal path to Forte de la Latte (see left), and on round to Cap Fréhel.

FORT LA LATTE

*Magnificent views in the
area. Rare mediterranean
plants, lush vegetation.*

4Km
1

Between Fort de la Latte and Erquy (see p. 45), be careful to stick to the GR, not trampling on the vegetation or taking short-cuts which could harm the natural surroundings. The path from Fort de la Latte to Cap Fréhel is a botanist's dream, with bracken, brambles, hawthorn and blackthorn on the rich soil; low gorse and heather on the sandstone at Fréhel. The GR then comes to Cap Fréhel.

CAP FRÉHEL
✕ ♟ ⛴

*With its 70 metre cliffs of
pink sandstone, it is a
popular place to visit. Many
different types of sea birds
nest on the sheer rock faces
in April and May. The whole
sea has been designated a
nature reserve. The SEPNB
(Society for the Study and
Protection of Nature in
Brittany) has a small office
on the site to provide
information. The area is also
of great mineralogical and
botanical interest. You can
also visit the lighthouse.*

2.5Km
0:40

A narrow and rather precarious path runs half-way up the cliffs around the point at Cap Fréhel (see left). It provides very good observation spots, but can be dangerous in strong winds. The departure point for this path is behind La Fauconnière. The cliff-top walk around the point is also very spectacular.

The GR continues westwards from Cap Fréhel across a sandy moor to the Pointe du Jas, where there is also a hide for keen bird watchers at La Banche rock. Continue on above Port-aud-Sud-Est.

Port-au-Sud-Est
Detour, *15 mins*
LA VILLE-HARDRIEUX
⌂

4Km
1

The GR continues across the moor on the coastal path, and then drops down to the village of Pléherel-Plage.

PLÉHEREL-PLAGE
🏠 ✕ 🚉 🚌

Here, the GR makes a sudden turn inland over La Pointe aux Chèvres (Goat Point), and then takes the D34a right. Keep the quarries on

43

5Km
1:15

SABLES-D'OR-LES-PINS

4Km
1

POINTE DU CHAMP DU PORT

9Km
2:15

ERQUY

History relates the tale of a town swallowed up by the sea. Some call it Nazado and believe it is situated between

your right, and when you get to the top of the slope, head inland again. Keep well away from the quarries, as landslides are possible. The GR then cuts across the road, and heads through a wood to pick up the D34a again, where you turn left. Drop down to the right beside the fence until you reach the beach, where you should go left to Sables-d'Or-les-Pins.

When you get to the roundabout at the end of the sea front make your way left into the dunes and follow the coast. Take the D34a to the cluster of houses at La Gare, where you turn right and cross the River Islet on a disused railway bridge which is now in very bad condition. At the other side of the bridge turn right and head along the track to Vallée Denis: you take the road going north-west when you get there, to the Pointe du Champ du Port.

The GR runs alongside the campsite and over some large boulders to La Fosse Eyrand, a holiday centre. Drop down to Plage du Guen, and then make your way back up to the coastal path which wends its way along above Plage de Lourtais between two high fences: these mark a zone where the dunes are in danger, and efforts are being made to protect them. It then passes an old fountain, and takes a path overgrown with bracken and gorse to Le Cap d'Erquy.

The GR sets off again from the car park at Cap d'Erquy and follows the road for a few metres before diving into gorse and brushwood which leads towards La Pointe des Trois Pierres (Three Stones point), where you can see a kiln for manufacturing cannon balls. You then take a path overlooking old quarries, now called Les Lacs Bleus (the Blue Lakes), from where you have a good view over the harbour. Take the road again for a few metres and then follow the steps down to the sea front at Le Bourg beach in Erquy.

When you get to the fishing port of Erquy, follow the quay. A little further on, take a path on your left leading to the D786, and head right along it. After 500 metres, the GR turns right along a footpath to Plage de Caroual. Make your way along the shore, then take a

10Km
2:30

Cap d'Erquy and La Pointe de Pléneuf-Val-André. Others believe that the drowned city was Erquy itself. In the nearby hamlet of Tu-ès-Roc, the remains of two lines of fortifications have been uncovered. Called Camp de César (Caesar's camp), they probably date from the Gallo-Roman era.

coastguard path to Plage de Saint-Pabu. Stay on the road to La Ville-Berneuf, then take the coastguard footpath which overlooks Plage de Nantois. A little further on, you will cross the campsite and the car park at Les Vallées and come to Pointe de Pléneuf. The GR now drops down some steps to the harbour at Pléneuf-Val-André.

PLÉNEUF-VAL-ANDRÉ

4Km
1

At low tide, you can get to the island of Le Verdelet, which is a protected nature reserve for birds.

The GR follows the quays along the sea front at high tide, or runs along the beach when the tide is out. When you reach the end of the quay, follow the signpost left to the *Corps de Garde* (guardhouse), and then turn immediately right along a little street that takes you back to the coastguard footpath. This goes all the way to Dahouët.

DAHOUËT

3Km
0:45

Small fishing port and marina, sailing school.

The GR skirts round the port and heads right, over the bridge across the Flora estuary. When you get to the other side, turn right into the Quai du Murier (Mulberrybush Quay) and take the footpath that runs along the clifftop to Le Port-Morvan.

LE PORT-MORVAN

3Km
0:45

When you have passed the grocery at Le Port-Morvan, take the road on your right (marked *sans issue* — dead end) and then drop down the paved path to the sea. Just before you get to the beach turn left along the clifftop path which leads to the car park at La Cotentin beach.

LA COTENTIN

The village itself lies off the GR.

1Km
0:15

Detour, *45 mins*
PLANGUENOUAL

The unusual Vaujoyeux dovecote, with its four towers, dating from the 16th century is well worth a visit.

The GR skirts La Cotentin, crossing the car park and continuing along the path opposite, which runs between the cultivated fields and the shore. You will now drop steeply down to the beach at Jospinet.

JOSPINET

The GR crosses the road and the little stream, and then continues along the path at the edge of the cliff. After a few kilometres you drop towards the creek at Le Pont-Rouault. Pass the

Detour, *15 mins*
LE VAL
⌂ ✕

5Km
1:15

There is a manor house, and the Saint-Marc chapel nearby, with an altar-piece dating from the late 17th century.

Le Pont-Rolland
Detour, *15 mins*
Morieux

Norman church with an alternating grey and redstone façade.

10Km
2:30

L'Hôtellerie

Detour, *10 mins*
HILLION
Ⓗ ▲ ✕ ⛟ ▭

Church dating from the 13th and 14th centuries.

4Km
1

water course before climbing up, still on the clifftop, towards the ruins of Saint-Maurice chapel, cross the approach road and the car park. The GR takes you to the top of the Gouessant river-mouth, where you make your way up the path that runs through brushwood and gorse to a meadow. Skirt this, then drop down through woods, cross a water course and you will come to Le Pont-Rolland.

Cross Le Pont-Rolland and, on arriving at a bend in the road 200 metres later, head right into the undergrowth. Ford the little stream and then take the path almost opposite which wends its way through woodland beside the sea. Continue until you reach a meadow. Follow a fence and skirt the fields until you reach a car park. You should cross this and stay on the path until you reach an approach road to Plage de La Granville. Cross this road and continue straight on, running along the right-hand side of an estate. You drop down to sea level again as you cross the Bon Abri (Good Shelter) dunes. Take care to follow the signposts and to follow the bends. The dunes are an interesting geological feature and are nearly 5,000 years old.

On leaving the dunes, turn left for 50 metres. Turn right along the road just after the campsite, and follow this for 150 metres before you rejoin the sea-shore as you pass the edge of a field. Continue along to Lermot beach, and then cross a car park back to the path. Make your way through a sheep fold, taking care to shut the gates. When you come to the steps leading to the beach, make for the clifftop straight ahead. After a short while you will pass two block-houses. Continue until you reach the shore at Saint-Guimont. The GR continues straight along the coastline to L'Hôtellerie.

Continue along beside the sea for a short distance, and then take the path through the grasslands until you emerge onto the shore. Climb to the top of a small road, take the wooden steps back up to the top of the cliff, and make your way alongside fields and woodlands. After about 2 kilometres, the path joins up with a small road at Pisse-Oison. Take this, and turn right at the next junction. The road bends sharply to the left beside a dike

YFFINIAC

10Km
2:30

Plérin (Le Legué)
Swing-bridge

Detour, *45 mins*
SAINT-BRIEUC *(centre)*

which gradually becomes overgrown with grass. At the next junction, turn right towards Yffiniac. At the junction with the D10, turn right, away from the town.

The GR continues along beside the sea for several kilometres, passing through Bourienne and Le Rivage. At Bout de Ville, turn off the road to the right along a path, formerly a railway track. Turn right alongside the fence of the hut. You then start to climb again, as you cross a gorse meadow, skirt a field and continue until you reach a street. Turn right for 150 metres, and then turn right again along a footpath which meanders through the houses and rejoins the coastguard footpath. Drop down the steps and then climb up onto the dike: you now continue along past the beach huts. When you have passed some more steps, turn right and follow the path which plunges into the undergrowth. You have a good view of Légué port and the bay. When you get to the port, turn left and pass the locks to a junction with a local GR, marked in yellow and red (an unnumbered GR de Pays). From here continue to the Plérin swing bridge near St Brieuc (10 Km, 2:30). If you want to go into the centre of St Brieuc, however, you should follow the yellow and red markings of this GR de Pays. The GR34 coast path can be rejoined later either here or a little further along at the Plérin swing bridge.

The GR34 now makes its way to the Plérin swing bridge.

Alternative route for joining the coast path from Saint-Brieuc. Turn right along Boulevard Charner as you come out of Saint-Brieuc station, and then cross Boulevard Clemenceau at the traffic lights and make your way along Boulevard Waldeck-Rousseau until you reach La Rue du Combat des Trente (Street Where the Thirty Fought). There are traffic lights here as well.

Take the steps on your left and follow the passageway which comes out at Rue de Gouedic. Cross this street and turn into Le Chemin de Belle-Isle (Beautiful Island lane) which drops down towards Gouedic Valley.

4Km
1

Follow the road along beside the left bank of the River Gouedic (it has recently been remade) and you will pass under Armor bridge.

When you reach the sports ground, take the tree lined dirt track on the left, and follow the fence at the other end which leads to a wooden underground tunnel. Go through this and turn left along the path that follows the right bank of the river immediately afterwards. This takes you underneath Toupin bridge. When you come to a tree lined dirt track, make sure you keep it on your right while you drop down again towards the Gouedic. You will come to another dirt track and then a paved lane which runs along beside the water purification station (on your left) to Surcouf quay.

Make your way along the quay to the swing-bridge and cross it. On your left, you will see the recently constructed viaduct (1979) which forms part of the Paris–Brest road. You now come to Plérin swing-bridge.

**Plérin (le légué)
swing-bridge**

On your left you meet up with the local GR to Loudéac (this in turn joins up with the GR371).

Detour, *via local GR route to*
BOIS BISSEL
⌂

Detour, *30 mins*
Plérin centre
Monolithic celtic cross near the church. In the church is the figure of the 17th century Thébault de Tanouarn recumbent on his tomb.

3.5Km
0:50

The ruins of Cesson tower from the 11th and 14th centuries are built on the site of a Roman encampment.

After you have crossed the swing-bridge, head right along the quay. You will come to the commercial part of the port first, and then to the area where the oil tankers dock. You will now come to Plérin (Saint-Laurent-de-la-Mer).

**PLÉRIN
(Saint-Laurent-de-la-Mer)**

When you get to the end of the quays, turn off the road which climbs up to the left and take the lighthouse road. You should climb the steps which you will find on your left just before the lighthouse, and follow the path on the right, which is actually the coastguards' footpath. You can see Saint-Brieuc bay from

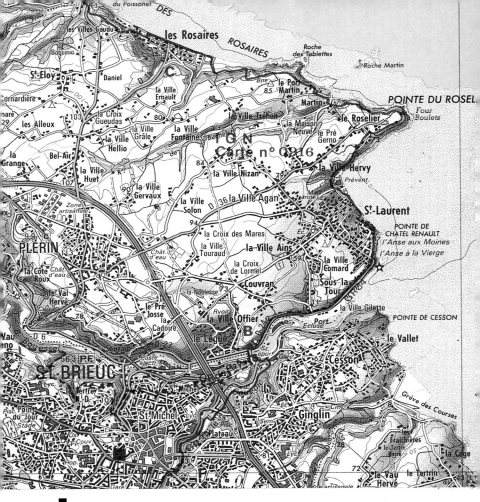

2.5Km
0:40

the car park. Follow the footpath along L'Anse aux Moines (Monks' Cove) and La Rue des Trois Plages and then drop down the land leading to the beach before turning left along the lane which follows the promenade along the shore. Turn left at the end of the promenade and then right along Le Chemin Saint-Jean until you get to La Rue Docteur-Violette. You should turn left here and then right again along the street which passes the solar-marine station. Turn off this remade track after about 500 metres, and take the lane on your right. From here, you have a good view of Plérin, Légué harbour mouth, Saint-Brieuc and L'Anse d'Yffiniac as you walk towards Pointe de Roselier

Pointe de Roselier

Here you can see a kiln for manufacturing cannon balls which dates from the time of Napoleon. Views over Saint-Brieuc bay towards Le Val André in one direction, and over Saint-Quay-Portrieux in the other. La Roche Saint-Martin is in the foreground.

4Km   **MARTIN-PLAGE**
1

Take the path along the clifftop to Martin Plage, making sure all the while not to follow any of the paths on your right down to the sea or to the various waterside properties. You should take care, as there are occasionally

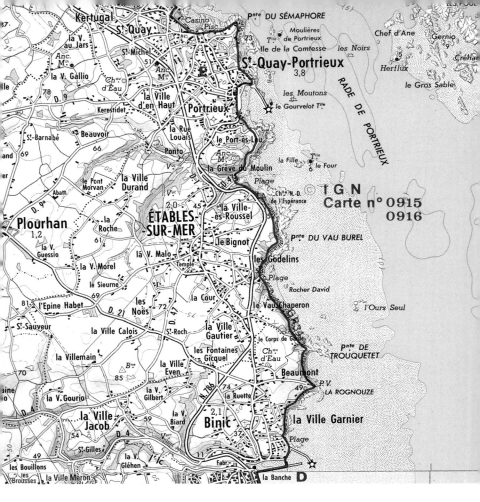

landslides in this area.

Follow the road on your right, leading to Port Martin, for about 400 metres, then turn right along a lane before heading left along the clifftop path. Climb over the wire-netting fence and then make your way towards the sea until you come to a wall. Skirt around the wall keeping it on your left until you reach the shore, and continue to Les Rosaires.

Walk all the way along the promenade at Les Rosaires, take the last street on the left, and then La Rue des Horizons on your right. This eventually turns into a path which continues all the way to Tournemine.

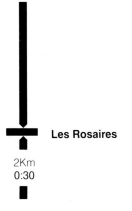

Les Rosaires

2Km
0:30

Tournemine
Detour, *50 mins*
PORDIC
(H) ⛺ 🍷 ⛴ 🚌

7Km
1:45

BINIC
(H) ⛺ ✕ 🍷 ⛴
🚌 i

4.5Km
1:10

Take a right turn off the road along La Rue Ronsard and follow the street to the end. Turn left and then right along a lane about 50 metres later, and then take the path opposite. You stay on this until you come to a look-out point which gives you a view out over Tournemine. Take the path on your left and then turn right at the crossroads along a road which narrows to a small track. Make your way into the small wood on your left, and you will eventually come to the car park at Le Petit-Havre. Continue along the higher footpath, rather than dropping down any of the paths on the right which lead to the waterside. You will come to Port-Madec (not labelled on map), the end point of a deep valley, near Pointe de Bréhin. Cross the stream and take the second path on your left, which you follow to the outlying houses. Turn right off this path along the track leading to Binic.

Take the street on your left, and stay on this until you reach the road on the right: this comes out on the promenade and La Banche car park.

Follow the promenade until you come to the *syndicat d'initiative* building. Turn along the quay on the right which makes its way round the port, and then cross the swing bridge and the right quay to the steps which begin just before the passage down to the beach. Keep the jetty on your right. The GR keeps to the upper road without turning off down the paths to the shore. From here, you have a view along the beach, and over Binic jetty and the coast towards La Pointe du Pordic. Take the path on your left — make sure you don't drop down to Rognouze on the right-hand track by mistake. From here you can see to La Pointe du Roselier, and if the weather is fine, as far as Cap Fréhel. Continue on until you come to La Pointe du Trouquetet. Drop down onto the point, and then climb up again along the right-hand track towards the houses. When you come to the steps, take the sunken path on your left. Half-way up this, you should take the steep slope which climbs up to the hillock on the right. At the hillock, leave the old campsite behind and take the dirt track to the first street on your right, the Rue des Roches Brunes (Brown Rock street), which turns into a path and then takes some steps up to the top road

© I G N
Carte n° 0815·0915

Les Godelins
Detour, *20 mins*
ÉTABLES-SUR-MER

3Km
0:45

From here, you can see along the coast to Fréhel. Notre-Dame de l'Espérance chapel, a sea-farers' church dating from the 19th century.

on the left. From here you take the steps down to the beach car park at Les Godelins.

Head upwards along the road on your left and take the path which leads out of the right-hand side of the second car park. Make sure you keep the steps on your right. Carry on past the chapel (see left), and take the path on your right which runs along beside the restaurant in Chemin de la Colombière (Dovecote Lane). This takes you past a cross, and down to the beach at Le Moulin. Cross the access road leading to the beach, and continue along the street until you come to a small road on your right which you should follow until you come to the quay at Portrieux harbour.

PORTRIEUX
ⓗ ✕ ℉ ⚓ 🚌

3Km
0:45

SAINT-QUAY
ⓗ ⚠ ℉ ⚓ 🚌

3Km
0:45

Saint-Marc
The old chapel was partly reconstructed in the 18th century.

Detour, *25 mins*
TRÉVENEUC
ⓗ ✕ ℉ ⚓ 🚌

4Km
1

Picturesque Breton church, with altar-piece and 18th century statues; fine grounds of Pommorio Château.

LE PALUS
℉

Detour, *1 hr*
PLOUHA
ⓗ ⚠ ✕ ℉ ⚓
🚌

6Km
1:30

The harbour, quays and promenades of Portrieux harbour take you along beside the sea to Saint-Quay.

Climb up the steps past the casino and Palais de Congrès (Conference centre), and follow the upper road to La Pointe de L'Isnain. Take the steps to the remade lane and turn off immediately along the path which meanders along beside the cliffs (ignore the various other paths that you will come across). You will then arrive at the beach and chapel at Saint-Marc.

Take the lane on your right again, and turn off this when it bends left and follow instead the path leading to La Pointe du Bec de Vir. Stay on this path until you come to the car park, and pick it up again at the bottom right of the car park. Keep the steps down to the beach on your right, and continue along the path around the fields, which are private property. Take the surfaced track on your right until you come to the second crossroads. Follow the sunken lane opposite and turn right onto the road. Turn off this road onto a dirt track which will take you to the beach at Le Palus (F on map).

Make your way along the beach until you come to the car park.
Climb the steps which you will see to the right of the café, and follow the path which heads inland underneath the pine trees. As you begin to climb, turn right back towards the coast again and follow the shoreline closely. When you come to a house, turn right to La Pointe de Plouha (not labelled on map), from where you have a good view of the surrounding area. Stay close to the shore and make your way round the point of Le Pommier (Apple Tree Point) past the campsite. You will come to a tarmacked road, and you should turn right along this to La Pointe de Gwin Zégal.

Retrace your steps upwards and then take the path on your right which leads to the car park and the beach at Port Moguer. Make your way up the path opposite, turn right after the second house and then take a small path on your right which leads to a stele. This marks a spot which was vital during the war to the Resistance as a departure point for Allies

Plage Bonaparte

3.5Km
1

pilots making their way over to England. Turn left 50 metres later along the small path that drops down to the car park at Plage Bonaparte.

Cross the car park and take the path opposite. As you climb up, turn sharp right, carry on along the coastline and then turn right after the second loop. You will come to La Pointe de la Tour. Continue round the curve of the point and follow the coastline before turning right and dropping down to the shore.

Cross the stream and follow the path which climbs up on your left towards a wood. The path gradually becomes a dirt track and skirts the fields. From here, you have a good view of the port of Bréhec and the beach. You will come to a crossroads, where you join up with the GR341.

Junction with the GR341
Detours: *10 mins*
KERJOLIS
⌂
10 mins
LANLOUP
Ⓗ ✕ ⚓ 🚌
Church dating from the 15th and 16th centuries.

1Km
0:15

When you get to the crossroads, the GR34 takes the track on the right. It turns left along a footpath when it reaches the half-way car park and makes its way along the old railway track. When you get to the old station, turn right along a path and take the steps down to the beach. Head left at this point towards Bréhec car park.

BRÉHEC
Ⓗ ⛺ ✕ ⚓ 🚌

From Bréhec onwards, some of the signs and markings may change from time to time as rights of way are restored beside the sea. Keep your eyes open for signposts. Head along the beach, and take the coastguard's footpath along the cliff, which starts behind the newspaper shop. When you reach the first outcrop, continue straight on to the holiday route, and follow it for 1 kilometre. Take the path on your right down to Porz Pin, and climb up the path which starts opposite the car park and runs along the cliff, wending its way left towards the clifftop. Make your way round the left-hand side of a conifer plantation, and as you approach the windmill turn along the road on your right to La Pointe du Minard. Just to the north of this point, the GR heads inland and takes the paved track on the right after the crossroads.

12Km
3

Head along the path on the right which skirts the fields and drops down to Porz Donan. You should then climb up the path opposite and continue along the cart track. Turn right at L'Armorizel, and make for La Pointe de Plouézec. Shortly before the point, the GR drops down to the left along a path which heads inland. Follow the road when you get to the car park and turn right to Port Lazo.

PORT LAZO
✕

From here the coastal path is being restored, and you may find changes in the route. Follow the signposts carefully. The GR climbs up the road on the right, bending sharply left to the crossroads at Saint-Riom.

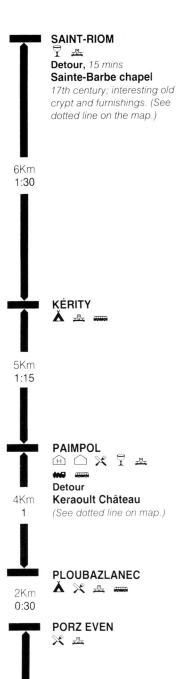

SAINT-RIOM

Detour, *15 mins*
Sainte-Barbe chapel
*17th century; interesting old
crypt and furnishings. (See
dotted line on the map.)*

6Km
1:30

KÉRITY

5Km
1:15

PAIMPOL

Detour
Keraoult Château
(See dotted line on map.)

4Km
1

PLOUBAZLANEC

2Km
0:30

PORZ EVEN

Turn sharp right along the road, and at Kervor, drop down to the shore at Boulgueff (not labelled on map).

The GR turns left along the shore at Boulgueff, and climbs up to the left by means of steps hewn out of the cliff. Continue along the shoreline until you come to the car park at Kérarzic. Take the path opposite the oyster bed buildings which climbs up to the left. You will subsequently drop down into a ravine, where you should take the track on your left and cross the stream on your right. Continue along the path opposite, keeping the ruins of Abbaye de Beauport on your left, and stay on the road which runs along beside the sea to Kérity.

At Kérity beach, take the path beside the sea to the tidal mill, where you turn left along the dike to the public gardens. The GR continues along beside the sea until it comes to the shore at Kernoa (Kerdrez). Here, steps ascend beside a house, climb these and then follow the coastguard path to La Pointe de Gilben. The GR runs parallel to this part of the northern coast until it gets to Tossen (not marked), on the outskirts of Paimpol harbour.

Make your way round the harbour, and then round the edge of the bay to Les Salles Château. Continue along the shoreline and then along the small path. You can climb Tour de Kerroc'h (Kerroc'h Tower) on your left. When you reach the small road, continue on past the first crossroads and turn left at the cross. Cross the D789 and continue on to the church at Ploubazlanec.

Turn right opposite the cemetery, cross the D789 again and continue straight on until you come to Porz Even.

Turn along the path leading left out of the harbour to La Chapelle de la Trinité, and after the chapel continue along the coast. Near to La Croix des Veuves (Widows' Cross), the GR takes a road on the right. At the transformer, turn right along a path leading to the shore at

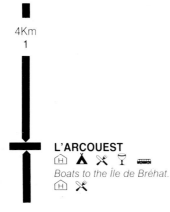

4Km
1

L'ARCOUEST

⌂ Ⓧ ✕ ☖ 🚌

Boats to the Île de Bréhat.

⌂ ✕

Launay. Turn right off the road, and then left along the shore for about 500 metres before climbing up the track opposite. Turn right along a wide path and then, after 50 metres, left along a track edged with broom. Continue along the paved lane. When you reach the road, turn right. At the first crossroads, you should turn left and take the path on your right which leads to the landing stage at Pointe de l'Arcouest.

From here head up the road again, cross the car park on the right, and then make your way along the shore, following lane or shingle as appropriate. After you have passed the large

6Km
1:30

LOGUIVY-DE-LA-MER
✗ 🚉 🚌
A pretty fishing port.

10Km
2:30

Detour,
Keraoult Château
(See dotted line on map.)

rock, find your way round the left-hand side of two fields, keeping close to the hedgerows, and then follow the road on the right again. When you come to a crossroads, take the dirt track on your right and continue on until you come to another road. Turn right. After passing a farm at a bend in the road, turn off right along a dirt track. Make your way right cross country until you reach the sea, and then make your way to the left along the shore. Continue along the road which climbs the hill. When you reach the house, continue almost straight on along the dirt track, and skirt the wall belonging to a large property. When you come to the road, take the lane opposite along past a maisonette, and then turn off along the road on your right which takes you to the sea. Follow the shoreline and continue along the road until you reach the harbour. Make your way round it until you come to the car park, and then turn along the road to the right to Loguivy-de-la-Mer.

Now head towards the point. When you come to a wall, turn left onto a winding road down to the sea, and then follow the coast. Climb up the road on the left again, and when you come to the top of the hill, take the road on your left. You now find yourself on a housing estate, and you should turn right into a dead end street.

Take the path that starts between two houses, and when you come to the far end, turn right onto the coastal path. When you reach the shore, turn left and follow the coast then take the path opposite which runs alongside the Trieux estuary departing only here and there from the line of the river. About 200 metres before you reach Coz Castel, drop down to the shore and climb up onto a dike. At Coz Castel itself, turn left and then immediately right along a field behind one of the houses. Head through the undergrowth beside the Trieux estuary again. Take the road on your left just before the *École d'Apprentissage Maritime* (Marine College) at Trieux. Continue on past Kerloury and La Rue Kéralain.

When you come to the crossroads which take you to Maudez, turn right then left along a lane. Turn right into the wood and drop down to the Trieux estuary, which you follow. At the

edge of the wood, head up to the left and when you reach the top of the slope, turn right. Turn right at the wash-house, and you will come out on the D786, where you turn right again. Cross the bridge, where the road bends right, into Lézardrieux.

LÉZARDRIEUX

🏠 ⛺ ✕ 🪑 🚌

Turn right after the church along the D20 to Lanmodez. Pass through the village of Kermenguy and then turn right at the cross-roads towards Coat-Min. Turn right again, then left along a dirt track after a farm, and drop down into a wood. You will come out at Coatmer (or Coatmed), where you can walk out to the point. Head past the tidal mill at Coatmer, and then follow the road linking the GR34 to the D20. Turn right. After a short distance, you come to Croaz-Rozel, where you veer right along another road to the hamlet of

11Km
2:45

TY-GUEN
⌂

4Km
1

LANROS
⚑ ⚲

Experimental seaweed
factory, investigating the
possibility of industrial
cultivation of seaweed and
other algae. Open to the
public on certain days.

3Km
0:45

Kerhamon. You can get to the estuary from here (see map). At Kerhamon, the GR heads north to Prat where it turns right along the Bodic road for 400 metres, then left along a dirt track which skirts a large estate. Shortly after this, it turns right along a path (you may have to follow the edge of the field if the path is overgrown). Make your way up the path opposite and then turn right along the tarmac lane through Kernarhant towards Kermouster. When you reach the edge of the village, take the path on your right which leads back to the road. The GR follows this road left for a few metres, and then turns right shortly before the Kermouster chapel. When you get to the top of the path, take the dirt track on your left. Turn left again in front of the farm and then right along the road (D20) on your right, and then turn off instead along the old road which runs alongside the right hand side of the main road. You will pass through Le Paradis and should turn right along the road just before the café. Turn right again and then left along a path which leads onto a tarmac road. When you come to Porz-Guyon, follow the coast road to Ty-Guen.

As you leave Ty-Guen, take the second turning on your right as far as the T-junction. Turn left, and then right at the second junction. When you come to the road, turn right to Goré after which you turn right again until you come to the sea. Head left through the furze when you come to the shore, keeping away from the wall. Turn right along a sandy track for a short distance, and continue along another path on your right. At the first house you come to, either take the cart track on your right along the shore, or, since the beach may be covered at very high tides, make your way along the lanes. The GR heads north for the D33 at Lanros.

Turn right along the D33 to La Pointe de Lanros (not labelled on map) and skirt round the seaweed plant (see left). Continue along the north coast until you come to the small hamlet of Le Québo.

LE QUÉBO
✗ ⍋
Detour,
L'ARMOR
🏠 ⛺ ✗ ⛴ 🚃

5Km
1:15

Kermagen
Detour, *30 mins*
PLEUBIAN
🏠 ⛺ ✗ ⛴ 🚃
Church with an exterior
sculpted pulpit.

Luzuret
Site of a prehistoric dolmen.

The GR runs along beside the sea and follows the coastal footpath to Porz Ran beach, which it crosses. At the end of the beach, you should make your way up the road on your left, and you will come to another road where you turn right to the fortress at Creac'h Maout, where there is a landmark indicator. Behind the ruins of the old signal station, you head down the heath. When you get to the bottom, cross the road leading to the shore and climb up the embankment which leads to a field. Follow the path round the edge of this field which looks out over the shore: it may be overgrown in places. Climb over the embankment leading away from the coast and head left to a tarmacked lane. When you come to a house, turn right along a path which drops down to the sea. Turn left along the shore, and you will find yourself starting to climb again as you make your way along a path overhanging the rocks. You now drop down onto the beach again and follow it to Port-la-Chaîne, where there is a campsite. Make your way past the lighthouse and continue along the edge of the shore until you come to a rocky point. You now climb up the path to the top and drop down the other side. If you follow the shore, you will come to the dock at Kermagen.

Head past the café at Kermagen, and take the route that runs along beside the sea. Continue along the shore past the campsite and follow the coastal path to Saint-Laurent. Here, head left along the dock and take the road on your left for 200 metres before turning right along a path. Turn right when you come to the road, and this will lead you to Port-Béni. Head left along the shore, and take the dirt track at the bottom of the bay and then right along the road, which subsequently narrows to a lane leading to the hamlet of Luzuret (see left).

At a fork in the road, the GR heads right towards the sea. Make your way along the shingle and turn off along the first lane on your left, then head along the path to your right. You will come out on a road which you follow right to Kerlizou. When you see a house on a bend in the road, take the track on your right. This takes you to Bellevue, where you should turn right along the road. You then take a left fork shortly before you come to the sea, dropping

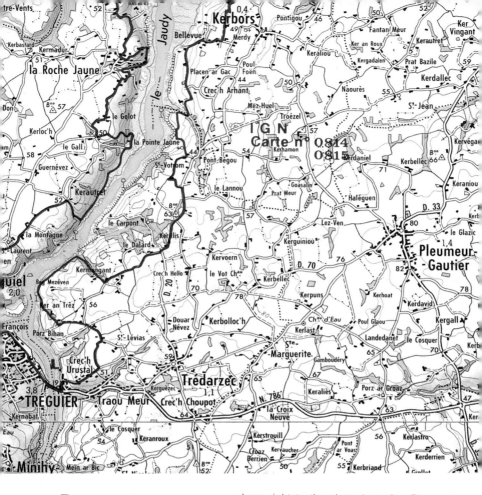

15Km
3:45

down right to the shore just after Placen-Ar-Gac.

Continue along the shore until you come to an old house. Just before this house, turn left along a path leading to Saint-Votrom chapel. Pass the chapel and turn right along a grassy track to a farm, and make your way round the left-hand side of it. You then take a tarmacked lane to the D20, where you turn right. Turn off the D20 at Kerilis and take the small road opposite. Turn right when you come to a crossroads and follow the wall running round the farm. Make sure you keep Kermangant on your left. As you begin to drop down, turn along a small overgrown track which meanders down to the sea. Follow the estuary, and then turn left along a lane which climbs back up to Ker an Trêz. Go through the village, and then turn left and immediately right along a dirt track. When you reach the road, turn right and make your way to Saint-Lévias.

The land which bends left, and at Crec'h Urustal turn right along a road leading to the River Jaudy. Here, you turn first left and then right across Tréguier swing bridge.

TREGUIER

When you have crossed the bridge, make your way round the port. Turn left past Saint-François bridge and then immediately right into a wood (Poet's Wood). Follow the foot-bridge across the River Guindy, and then turn immediately left and then right along the slope. Turn left along the D8 and when you come to the Souvenir de Mission cross, turn right along the small road. When you come to another cross, make your way towards Saint-Laurent chapel. Continue through La Montagne (the mountain) and head for the hamlet of Kerautret, where accommodation is available. Turn right there, along a track which drops down to the Jaudy. When you reach a group of four houses, follow the course of the river (which may be impossible at high tide) until you come to a small harbour. Continue on to La Pointe Jaune (Yellow Point), and once you come to the shore, turn left along a path after the last house. When you reach a transformer, turn right along the road towards the market town of La Roche Jaune (Yellow Rock). Before you reach it, turn right along a remade track, close to a farm, then left along a dirt track close to a stone cottage: the latter part of this track has also been remade. At the top of the lane, drop down to the right, towards the port. At the port, opposite the entrance to the beach, turn off left along a little street which runs between two houses near a fountain. This street will take you to the top of the village, where there is an observation tower on the right. You then retrace your steps towards La Roche Jaune.

Tréguier is an ancient diocese, owing its origins to a 6th century monastery founded by Saint Tugdual. Cathedral, dating from the 13th–15th centuries with tomb of Saint Yves (1253–1303), whose death is commemorated on 'Grand Paradis' day (19th May), tomb of the Breton ruler Jean V (1389–1442); monument and birthplace (now museum) of Ernest Renan, the French writer (1823–92).

9Km
2:15

LA ROCHE JAUNE

As a right of way is now being restored along the shore, you will soon be able to follow a coastal footpath between La Roche Jaune and Beg (or Begar) Vilin (beyond Plougrescant), so watch out for the signposts. When you come to the bus stop, turn right towards Lann Huit (not labelled on map), cross the Baie de L'Enfer

3Km
0:45

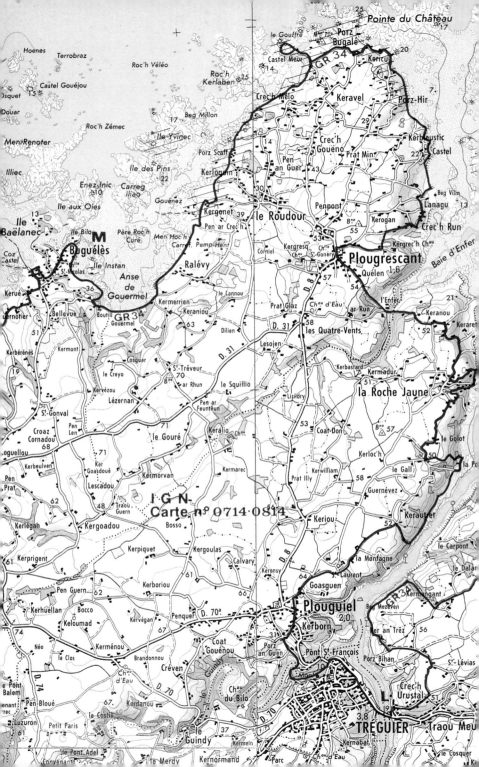

(Hell bay) by the bridge, and shortly afterwards, turn right along a lane which leads to the chapel of Saint-Gonéry at Plougrescant.

PLOUGRESCANT

ⵣ

Having come from Great Britain in the 6th century, Saint Gonéry came here to die after a long period in central Brittany. Saint Gonéry's tomb in curious chapel with leaning steeple and panelling decorated with 15th and 16th century pictures. In spring each year, saint's shrine carried to island of Loaven, 3 kilometres away, where his mother Eliboubane is buried.

12.5Km
3:10

PORZ-HIR

Detour, *10 mins*
CREC'H GOUENO

BUGUÉLÈS

16th century St Nicholas chapel

4Km
1

Turn right along the road just after Saint-Gonéry chapel. At the first fork, turn right and then drop down to the left along a tarmacked road. Turn right at the next road which will take you to Beg Vilin, where there is a campsite. You then follow the Chemin de Servitude (Bondage Lane) along the coast past Castel and Kerbleustic. At the foot of Porz-Hir, take the road on your right beside the sea and, after you come to the car park, follow the edge of the meadow. The GR then bends slightly away from the coast. This part of the coastal footpath is being restored and you will head round the Pointe du Château on the GR — so be sure to follow the signs. The road on your right will take you to La Pointe de Castel Meur.

The GR follows a path along the shore, passes a house with a white gable and continues to Porz Scaff. Here, you turn right along a path, left and then right again along the tarmac road which leads to Kerloquin. At Kergonet, turn right towards the coast, and then head along beside the sea past Ralévy, following either the shore or the path that runs parallel to it, and you will come to Anse de Gouermel (Gouermel Cove). Follow the road and, shortly after the beach at Boutill (not labelled on map), take the path on your right. The GR then runs along the shore until it reaches the jetty, and carries on into Buguélès.

The GR makes its way along the path opposite Saint-Nicholas chapel, and then turns right. Turn left when you come to the road. At the first crossroads, turn right and follow the tarmac lane for about 1 kilometre, then turn right along a track which drops down to Anse de Pellinec (Pellinec Cove) and go across it. Make your way along the coast and then turn left along a path after a house. Then take the small road on your right looking out for a villa 'Gwell Armor', where you drop down to the right towards the sea. Head along the path on your left and skirt the fields that roll down to the sea until you come to the jetty at Port-Blanc. You now climb up the road again and turn right to make your way across Port-Blanc.

73

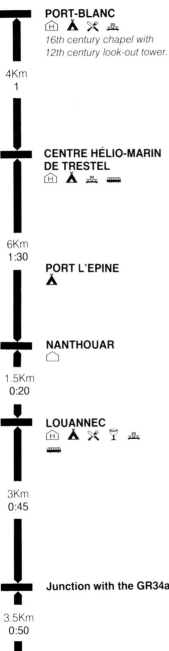

PORT-BLANC

16th century chapel with 12th century look-out tower.

4Km
1

CENTRE HÉLIO-MARIN DE TRESTEL

6Km
1:30

PORT L'EPINE

NANTHOUAR

1.5Km
0:20

LOUANNEC

3Km
0:45

Junction with the GR34a

3.5Km
0:50

Take the road that runs along beside the sea and, where it bends inland, follow the dirt track past Crec'h Avel into the dunes and Marais Launay (Launay Marshes). The route takes you along beside the shore at Le Royau, where there is a campsite, and this narrows to a lane before crossing the beach underneath the cliffs. Continue along the dirt tracks until you come out at the beach below the Centre Hélio-marin (Trestel solar-marine centre).

Take the D38 along the Plage de Trestel and then head right towards Port Le Goff. Continue on beside the sea and take the first turning on your left, and, at the edge of a conifer wood, turn right. You then skirt a field and continue along the lane. You subsequently turn left and then right before making your way over the shingle to Port L'Epine.

Cross the car park and take the lane running at right angles to the sea. Make your way over two fields and a meadow then follow the coastguard's path beside the sea for about 1 kilometre. At the road, turn right to Nanthouar.

Go past the lighthouse for about ½ kilometre, and turn along the dirt track on your left which subsequently becomes a tarmac lane. Turn right and then right again, and continue straight on to the church at Louannec.

Take the road which starts opposite the church at Louannec and heads towards Le Croajou. When the road bends to the right, 300 metres later, continue straight on along a lane which becomes paved. Turn successively right, left, right and right again in front of a farm. You now cross a road and take an unmarked path to Barach Château. When you reach the château turn right, and then left at the end of the path before continuing on to a paved lane on your right. At this junction, you meet up with the GR34a.

The GR34 follows the paved lane on the right. It continues straight on (north) across the next road it comes to, then after a few hundred metres it bends left (west) and back across the same road again. It passes along the foot of a slope and comes out at Pont-ar-Sauz, following the sea front all the way to Perros-Guirec.

PERROS-GUIREC

🏠 ⛺ ✕ ⛴ 🚂
❓

*One of the most beautiful
churches in Brittany; 12th
century nave and bas-côtés,
extended in Gothic style in
14th century; geometrical
capitals on two Norman
columns depict an Old
Testament scene.*

At the port, make your way between the wet
dock and the small lake, and continue along
the D788D. You then take the right fork along
the road to Trestignel and right again 100
metres later along the track marked *voie sans
issue* (dead end) which leads to the beach.
Make your way along the beach, and at the
other end climb up the steps on the left. Turn
left, and then right along Rue de Pré-Saint-
Maur. Continue on upwards for about 500
metres until you come to the crossroads, and
then turn right along La Rue Maurice-Denis
which leads to La Pointe du Château. The GR

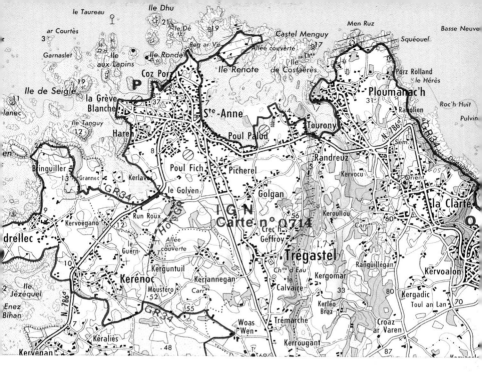

11Km
3

12th century Saint-Guirec chapel, dedicated to Saint Guirec (Kireg). The granite structure replaces a wooden statue where unmarried girls used to stick a pin into the saint's nose. If the pin didn't fall out, they knew they would soon be married!

PLOUMANAC'H

then runs along Trestignel beach. On leaving the beach, you make your way along Boulevard de Trestignel and Chemin de la Messe, and then turn left along Rue Anatole-France. Continue along Rue des Sept-Iles and turn right along Rue Maréchal-Foch which leads to Trestraou beach. Skirt the beach, and continue along the road to La Clarté. When the road takes a sharp bend to the left, turn off along the coastguard's path on your right at Kerdu. The track continues across rocks, where it is unmarked, and comes out at the beach at Ploumanac'h. Make your way across it.

Go along a path which leads past the chapel of Saint-Guirec, and then climb up onto a large pile of rocks. You then turn left and pass underneath an arch of shrubs and bushes before skirting a small beach and climbing up steps to a lane leading to a crossroads. Here you turn left through a pine forest and across a heath, and then left again along a road which leads to the port of Ploumanac'h.

Take the dike leading away from the first tidal mill, and continue on until you come to the

Detour, *10 mins*
Golgan chapel

5Km
1:15

N786, where you turn right towards Tourony. When you have passed the second tidal mill, make your way round the right side of the port, and then turn first right and then left at Tourony, where there is a campsite. Continue in a westerly direction. At Poul Palud, skirt the sports ground erected on the marshes, keeping it on your left as you go.

If the tide is sufficiently far out, make your way along the shore to Sainte-Anne. If not, take the main road south; you should stay on the road only for about 500 metres before turning right along a small track leading to the quay at Sainte-Anne.

Detour, *(2 Km by boat)*
Île Renote
Boats leave from the right-hand jetty.

The GR34 now continues right along the road and then turns off along the first path on the right.

The GR now heads along a path opposite, crosses a beach, and eventually comes to another beach at Coz Porz-Trégastel.

COZ PORZ-TREGASTEL

Make your way along to the end of the beach, and then take the path facing you which leads to La Grève Blanche (White Shore). Continue along the beach until you come to the point and then follow either the shore or a small path alongside for about 2 kilometres, and cross the small stream. The path will continue on through the gorse and then cross the sandy shore to the back of the bay. You should then follow a paved lane for 100 metres which brings you out on the D788, beside a campsite.

Detour,
Kerguntuil
10Km
2:30
Neolithic site with a magnificent dolmen and an enclosed passageway housing a communal burial ground. Inside the passage are sculptures hewn out of the granite walls.

The GR now follows the D788. At the first junction, you should turn right, right again, and then left along the dirt track past Banguiller to the sea, where you take the path to the left. Shortly afterwards, you turn left again opposite Île Laouen along a lane, and follow the coast for several kilometres round the Landrellec peninsula, where there are campsites. After you have passed the first campsite you continue along the coast path. Make your way *through* the second campsite, and then follow either the coastal path or the shore until you come to the D788 again. Turn right along the road, and then left 50 metres later along a lane. You then take the first road on the right, then take the lane to the left a few hundred metres further on. This crosses a road, and takes you almost to Kérénoc.

KÉRÉNOC

(As a result of regrouping of lanes and tracks in this area, you may find changes in the GR route between Kérénoc and Penvern.)

At the next crossroads the GR34 turns right, and then follows the road. It takes the second land on the left to Woas Wen where it heads right. You will cut across the road again and take the path opposite. Make your way over the golf course, pass the barrier and continue along the path which meanders through the gorse. Turn left in front of the 14th century

79

7Km
1:45

This radar dome includes a mobile antenna over 50 metres high which has been receiving television programmes transmitted by satellite since 1962. It also receives information transmitted by geostationary satellites. Visits can be arranged.

Detour,
Gallic village and planetarium
(See dotted line on the map.)

PENVERN

7.5Km
2

A track on your left will take you to a panoramic viewpoint, where there is a guardhouse and a covered passageway.

L'ÎLE GRANDE

Saint-Samson chapel, and then take the first right turn. When you reach a cross, you should turn left and keep going for about ½ kilometre. You then turn right along a path at the crossroads (IGN ref 60). When you reach the road (about ½ kilometre), you will be able to see the CTS (Centre de Télécommunications Spatiales — Space Communications Centre) radar dome on your left (see left).

Turn right along the road, and you will plunge into a wood beside a small house. Follow the fence surrounding the CTS through the wood. At the other side, you cross a meadow, take the path opposite and then continue straight on along the lane. When you come to the road turn left and drop down to the cluster of houses at Pont-Coulard.

At Pont-Coulard the GR heads right (west) for several kilometres. When you have passed the menhir (standing stone), you turn off along the second tarmac lane on the left and cross the D21. The GR passes the chapel at Penvern.

Turn right just after the chapel and, after a few hundred metres, cross the D788, taking the D21 towards L'Île Grande (Big island). A small path on the right avoids a 200 metre stretch on the main road. You then cross the bridge to the island. On your left is the covered passageway at Prajou and another menhir.

After the bridge turn right and make your way along the shore past the rocks beside various private estates. When you have passed the sailing school, continue on along the coastal path to the far side of the island.

Continue round the west and south sides of the island along the path which has been worn down by the sea until you come to a fountain. Turn right and then right again into the built-up area at L'Île Grande.

Take the first small street on your right and then go along the shore. You then turn along a small lane on your left and then down the street on your right. Turn right along the D21 away from the island. Shortly after the bridge,

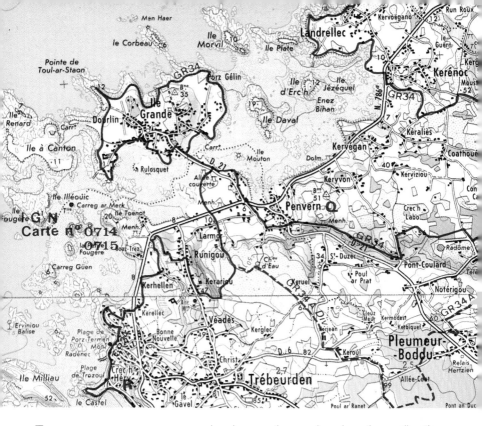

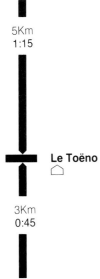

5Km
1:15

Le Toëno

3Km
0:45

head across the meadow along the small path which runs along beside the sea. It gets wider as it bends left. Cross the D788 and take the road opposite, and then the track leading to the top of the heath. At the top of the heath the GR34 turns right and runs down towards Kevariou. When you reach the next road, turn right (north) towards Runigou. Turn left after 500 metres, and then right along a path which leads to the D788. Turn left along the D788 past the Le Toëno youth hostel.

After 100 metres, cross the old quarry on your left. At the bottom of the quarry, you turn right along a path which leads to the road. Turn right, and then left along the D788. Turn left again after 150 metres and cross the D788. The second street on your right will take you round the Lan Kérellec peninsula. As you leave the peninsula, turn right along the coast. Two further right turns will bring you out at the port of Trébeurden.

TRÉBEURDEN

Menhir; dolmen; various covered passageways; chapel of Christ; Millau island; very good views from landmark indicator at La Pointe de Bihit.

7Km
1:45

BEG LÉGUER

9.5Km
2:30

LANNION

Many old streets and 15th and 16th century houses; 16th and 17th century Saint-Jean-de-Baly church; Brélévenez church (12th and 15th centuries) with its famous 142 steps, built by the knights Templars; the 15th century Saint-Roch chapel has a beautiful rood screen.

Loguivy-lès-Lannion

16th century church with sculpted 17th century altar-piece, enormous doors, 15th century fountain, and basined Renaissance fountain (1577).

At Trébeurden, the GR runs round the Pointe du Castel. It follows the shore at Tresmeur to La Pointe de Bihit. Continue along the coastal path, make your way round a field and then turn right. You should cross the road which drops down to Pors Mabo taking the small road opposite past a campsite. Turn right along the paved lane and then follow the coastal path for 3 or 4 kilometres to the car park at Beg Léguer.

Cross the car park and take the path which starts in the opposite corner. This runs along the coast and up beneath the lighthouse. You then drop down again to La Pointe de Beg Léguer and make your way round the point. The path twists and turns its way upwards, and comes out at a small lane, where you turn right. When you come to a roundabout, turn left and then right along a wall. Make your way round a meadow, and then turn right along a path which drops down to the river. When you come to a road turn left. Just before a bend in the road, you should turn off right along a lane which drops down to the river. Continue along the tow-path, which follows the Léguer inland for about 7½ kilometres, to the post office at Lannion. Cross the second bridge and take the third street on your left which brings you to the youth hostel at Lannion.

As you leave the youth hostel, take the Rue de Kérampont, and then continue along the road leading to Loguivy-lès-Lannion, which starts almost opposite. You will pass behind the cottage-industry zone and should carry straight on. Head right, down the hill and make your way past a pond and then a cross, and then drop down to the right to Loguivy-lès-Lannion.

Make your way past the church at Loguivy and continue straight on. Half-way up the hill, turn right along an overgrown track, and take the path that meanders across the heath. After journeying through woods and across meadows, you cross a stream and continue on across a meadow to Ruboêns farm. You then

8Km
2

4Km
1

3Km
0:45

3.5Km
1

head along the tarmac lane to the crossroads, where you turn right. Leave the road after a short distance, and drop down to the right along a sunken track which runs below a farm. You will join up with a lane which leads you back up to another road. Turn right to Kerdroniou farm. Make your way round the building, keeping it on your right, and continue straight on along the dirt track. Head right and drop down the steep overgrown path. The track on your left takes you underneath old oak trees and down to the river, where you follow the banks through thickets and copses. Make your way carefully past the barbed wire fence and head into the ferns before dropping down again to the river. The path sometimes runs along the riverbank, and sometimes meanders along at a higher level, looking down on the river. When you have passed the ruins of the ferryman's cottage, head right to the port and make your way round the peninsula along the shoreline. You then climb up to the left to the chapel of Le Yaudet.

LE YAUDET

This prehistoric site became a Gallo-Roman city (vetus civitas — old state) and then a Breton city called Coz Yeodet. Neolithic entrenchment which cuts across the spur; engraved rock on the crest is probably some sort of pre-celtic religious monument; there used to be a fortress (oppidum) up on the point; renaissance chapel with altar-piece depicting the Virgin and Child asleep.

Take the lane to the right of the chapel, and make your way round the point. You will come out on the road, where you should turn right and continue on to Le Pont Rous. Climb up the road on the right and after 250 metres turn left along the coastguard's path. When you come to an estate, make your way along a little track to the right which meanders between fence and embankment down to La Plage Carrée (Square Beach) (not labelled on map). You then head along the path which makes its way round La Pointe du Dourven. After the point, you come to a large field and continue along to the right under the cypress trees as you climb up to Plage du Notigou. You will come out on the D88A, where you should turn right to Locquémeau.

LOCQUEMEAU

16th century church.

Pass the sailing school and turn left along the road, which becomes a path when it reaches the cliffs. Shortly after La Pointe de Beg ar Néon, you join up with the GR34b.

Junction with the GR34b

The GR34 runs along the coast for several kilometres, until it comes to the jetty. It crosses the beach (or takes the small streets round it) to the church at Saint-Michel-en-Grève.

SAINT-MICHEL-EN-GRÈVE

(H) Å ✕ ⚓ 🚂

16th–17th century church.

10Km
2:30

Take the road on your right and, after a few hundred metres, turn off left along the path in front of the hotel. You will come out at the car park, where you should take the path immediately on your right and climb back up to the road again, beside the transformer. You then take the first lane on your left, and turn left again at the next-but-one track. When you have passed Kerarmet farm, turn down the dirt track which meanders along past a chapel. You then take the road on the left for a few metres before turning off right along a track which wends its way round the edge of a field. Take the common right of way across the next field, and continue along the path opposite which leads to Quatre Dames (farm). You then take the road left to Prat Kerléau. The GR34 takes the road on the right, and turns off right again along a lane when it comes to a house. It subsequently runs along beside a stream, crossing a meadow and then plunges into the undergrowth. You should turn left and then take the track on your right and drop down to the river. Cross the stone bridge. Head right along a track which bends left away from the river and makes a circular tour to Kéralio farm. Continue along the road, and turn first left and then right to Kerdudal. Cross over the D22 and continue on towards Coz Castel (not marked on map). The route makes its way past a farm and heads round the left hand side of a meadow. It then drops down into a copse and heads through the thicket to the River Yar, which it crosses. Climb up a path to the left and you will come out on the road not far from Kérameau (map ref T).

Alternative route Kérameau to Launay. This is the same distance as the GR34. At the first turning after Kérameau, turn left towards Coat an Iliz and Le Veuzit, and at the sharp bend in the road, turn right along the track leading to Pen an Nech. Climb up straight ahead towards the next farm (IGN ref 96), but heading instead left along a sunken track which runs below the farm track. When you reach the edge of the wood, go into the field opposite, and then turn right and enter the wood. Cut across a sunken lane and come out on another paved lane which leads to Launay farm, where you rejoin the GR34.

Just before Kérameau, the GR34 turns right along the road. When it reaches a spot just before the reservoir, in front of a small house, it turns left along a path. Take this path until you come to the signpost for Pont Ar Yar where you turn right. When you come to the road, turn off immediately along the path on the left which leads to the ruins of a maisonette. The path on the left will take you up to the top of the hill (IGN ref 84). From there, you should head right towards the big rock from where you have a good view along the coast and over the surrounding area. Go half-way round the rock, and then continue straight on along the crest via a somewhat overgrown path. You will come to a local footpath, and you should turn right and continue straight on until you come to Launay. A winding track will then take you to the D786. You should make your way round the house on your left, and turn off immediately along the road which runs almost parallel with the D786. This eventually narrows to a lane. When you have passed the old railway bridge, a right turn will bring you out on the D786 at Saint-Efflam.

SAINT-EFFLAM

Chapel; fountain reputed to be an oracle.

Turn right off the D786, and take the road that runs alongside the sea. Climb up the steps on the left into the wood, and then head through the wicket gate on your right. Make your way round the Toulinet *colonie de vacances* (holiday centre), and take the coastal path to La Pointe de Beg Douar. Continue towards Pointe de L'Armorique, and cross over the road. Head along the shore (southwards), past a campsite, and you will come to a meadow which has been turned into a car park where there is a hotel. Continue straight on until you come to a conifer hedge. Take the path which runs along beside the sea but never actually drops down to the beach. You will come out on the D42 opposite Sainte-Barbe chapel where you turn right along the D56, which leads to the port of Toul an Héry.

6Km
1:30

Toul an Héry
Junction with the GR34d.
Detour, *15 mins*
PLESTIN-LES-GRÈVES

Church dating in part from 15th century, housing the tomb of Saint Efflam; sacrificial stone (a sort of grooved stele); tumulus; remains of Gallo-Roman villas.

The GR runs over the bridge across the River Dourin, marking the boundary between Côtes-du-Nord and Finistère, and then turns along the first road on the right off the D64. It passes beneath the wall surrounding the Île Blanche (White Island) estate, and then heads round the cove and the sports ground over the dunes. Cross over the access road leading to the stadium and climb up the cliff. Take the path which leads to the beach access road. Drop down this for a few metres, and then turn along the passage which crosses the municipal campsite.

FOND DE LA BAIE

Cross over another access road leading to the beach. At low tide, you can get to Locquirec by simply walking along the coastline, but when the sea is in, you should fork left near to cypress trees at the back of the campsite. The path takes you to the D64, which leads to Locquirec.

4Km
1

89

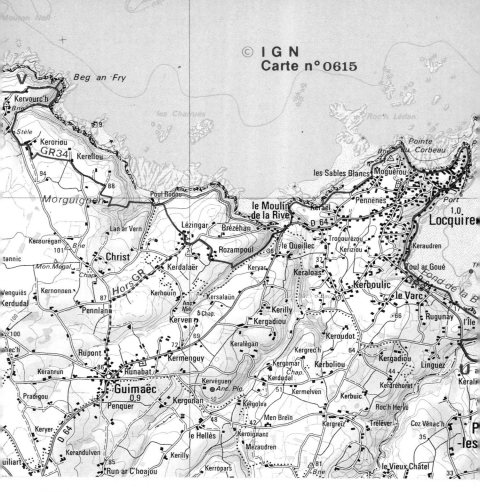

© **I G N**
Carte n° 0615

LOCQUIREC

🏠 🍴 ⚓

*Old Gallo-Roman seaside
resort. 14th and 15th century
church; 17th century
bell-tower; 16th century high
altar; 16th and 18th century
statues.*

4Km
1

La Pointe du Corbeau

*Good view of the
Trébeurden coastline (east)
and of La Pointe de Beg an
Fry (west).*

After the church, the GR turns right along the
first road it comes to, which leads to La Pointe
de Locquirec, and then on to the beach at
Pors ar Villiec. Climb up to the right on the
D64, and then drop down, again to the right,
opposite the dead-end at Pouldrein (not labelled). The path on the right will take you round
Saint-Kiren fountain. Turn right again and head
out to La Pointe du Corbeau (Raven Point).

The GR continues along the coastguard path
leading to Les Sables Blancs (White Sands
beach), where you make your way along the
wall separating the road and the dunes. You
will eventually come to the ruins of Moulin de la
Rive (Mill on the Shore).

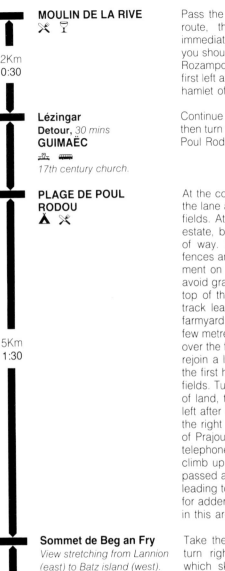

MOULIN DE LA RIVE

2Km
0:30

Lézingar
Detour, *30 mins*
GUIMAËC

17th century church.

PLAGE DE POUL RODOU

5Km
1:30

Sommet de Beg an Fry
View stretching from Lannion (east) to Batz island (west).

Pass the bar and turn right along the holiday route, then along the path on your left immediately afterwards. As you begin to climb, you should turn right along the path leading to Rozampoul. Take the local road, and then turn first left and then right until you come out at the hamlet of Lézingar.

Continue along the road from Lézingar and then turn first left and then right to the beach at Poul Rodou.

At the corner by the restaurant, turn left along the lane and then continue straight on to some fields. At this point, the GR crosses a private estate, but ramblers have been granted right of way. For this reason, please respect the fences and make your way along the embankment on the cultivated ground, taking care to avoid grazing land when cattle are on it. At the top of the meadow, the GR heads along the track leading to Morguignen farm. Cross the farmyard and turn right along the road. After a few metres, turn left along a track which heads over the fields. You pass a cypress hedge and rejoin a lane leading to Kerellou. Shortly after the first house, turn left along a track over the fields. Turn left when you come to the last plot of land, turn right at the track and then head left after Keroriou farm. Turn down the road to the right and, when you get to the tiny hamlet of Prajou, take the lane on the right after the telephone kiosk. Cross the picnic area and climb up the path on the left. When you have passed a marked rock, turn left along the path leading to the top of Beg an Fry hill. Watch out for adders here. There are also dangers of fire in this area.

Take the dirt track away from the point, and turn right shortly afterwards along a track which skirts a field. Make your way across Pont Melven farm (IGN ref 86), and then turn first left and then right along a road. A few hundred metres further on, head right along another lane. At the road, turn left along it, cross over the crossroads and head towards the wood. At the next main junction turn left and, when you come to the tiny hamlet of Le Croisic (not labelled on map), drop down to

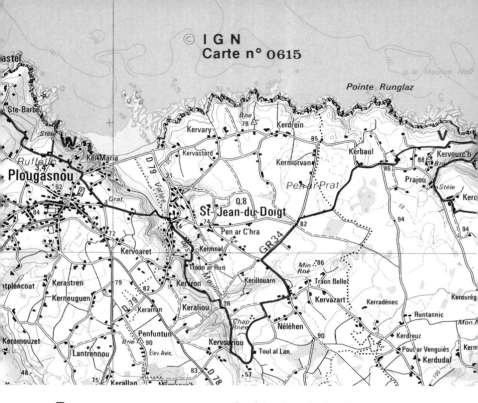

© **I G N**
Carte n° 0615

10Km
2:30

Saint-Jean-du-Doigt
*Church with delicate
prismatic columns
supporting a high wooden
arch (16.25 metres);
enormous apse window
crowned by magnificent 15th
century rose window; the*

the right along the local lane. Take the first left turn and then go right, along the path which leads to a renovated chapel. Continue on past Toul al Lan farm, then turn right along the lane into La Vallée des Moulins (Mill Valley). A little further, continue left. At the entrance to the meadow, turn left and then right towards Goris mill. Climb up to the left behind the buildings, and this will bring you out on the access road leading to the estate. Shortly after this, you should turn right along the lane which leads to Trégoladen (not labelled on map). Turn right along the road which bends sharply left at the fountain, and continues to Saint-Jean-du-Doigt (literally: Saint John with the finger).

The GR takes the beach road, runs along beside the cemetery and turns left along a lane at the last gate. Cross the bridge to Plougasnou.

tower lost its spire in a storm in 1925; ravaged again by fire in 1955; Duchess Anne founded it for pilgrims, after she was cured of an eye infection when touched by the relics of Saint Jean; oratory with bell turret which used to contain a light which threw shadows over the tombs; charnel-house; 15th and 16th century Gothic triumphal arch housing statues of St Jean and St Roch; attractive 17th century fountain; architecture is some of the most beautiful in Brittany; 16th century house, said to be the Maison du Gouverneur (Commanding Officer's home), has well preserved spiral stone staircase and Gothic front door.

1.5Km
0:20

PLOUGASNOU

15th and 17th century church; 16th century bell tower; Notre-Dame-de-Lorette oratory (1611) is a curious tomb-shaped stone building, the only one of its kind in the western world; inside, there is a 15th century statue of the Virgin Mother; cemetery with a marvellous coronation chapel with three gables (the only one of its kind in Europe) and 15th century octagonal pulpit, hewn from stone, crowned with a high cross.

Detour *if you turn off along the path a few metres before the manor house, you will come to a stele erected in memory of the Resistance fighters.*

The GR turns right immediately after the Notre-Dame-de-Lorette oratory. It runs round the edge of the cemetery and turns right at the first crossroads. Shortly afterwards, you should climb up the little street on your left which leads past Ruffélic manor house (map ref W).

When you reach the farm, turn left and then left again. Turn right at the road. Shortly afterwards, you should take the track on your left and then turn right along the road. The lane on your left will now take you past the chapel. Follow the road to the right and drop down to the beach. You should make your way over the beach to the steps leading to the coastguard's path along the cliffs. Skirt the campsite and you will come to La Pointe de Primel.

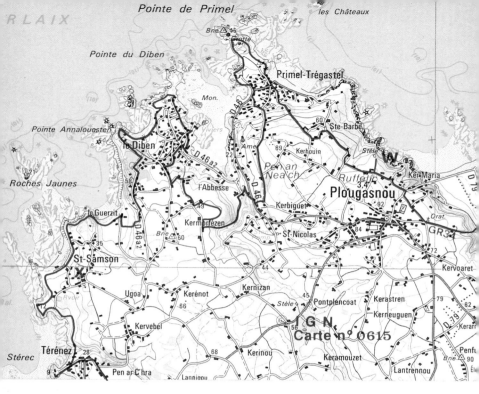

La Pointe de Primel

One of the most beautiful on the north Brittany coastline, with views of the wide open sea, the Seven Islands (now bird reserves), Batz island, Roscoff and Saint-Pol-de-Léon.

10Km
2:30

The GR is unmarked as it makes its way over this point.

Make your way along the edge of the coast. Cut across the D46 and then turn left along a local road which climbs up onto the plateau. Continue along the road towards the wood, and at a sharp bend in the road, take the path ahead of you which leads to Pen an Neac'h. When you get to the cross drop down to the right, and shortly after the bar, climb down the steps and cross over the D46 again. Make your way down the road on the right, which subsequently passes in front of Tromelin manor house. You should take the track on your left and climb up to the right shortly afterwards, to an area called *Jardin d'Amour* (Love Garden). You will now find yourself on a cart track. Veer left, on to the road at Kermorfézen. Head right and then left, and when you reach the next crossroads, turn right towards Le Diben. The road on your right will lead you to Port du Diben (Le Diben harbour).

Port du Diben
Fishing harbour

2Km
0:30

Cross the road and take one of the paths opposite which lead along the coast. You should then turn off along the lane leading to Port Blanc (White Harbour) Cove (not labelled on map). At the top of the beach, turn left along the path which meanders along at a higher level towards Pointe de Annalouesten. You pass an isolated estate and make your way round the point.

Pointe de Annalouesten

2Km
0:30

There may be slight changes in the route as the coastal right of way is being restored, so watch out for signs. Follow the road to the D46, and then turn right along it. When you have passed the sign indicating that you have now left Le Diben, head right to a house, and then right again along a path which brings you out on another road. Turn right to Guerzit beach.

Plage du Guerzit

1.5Km
0:20

Make your way along the wall around the property to your left and then continue on along the coast beside the fields and then a heath. The GR meanders along the cliff without turning off any of the paths on the left. You should cross two fields which have been turned into caravan parks and which are actually marked *Privé* (private). You can continue along this way as long as you are within 3 metres of the edge of the cliff. You will come out at the beach car park at Saint-Samson.

SAINT-SAMSON

2.5Km
0:40

Make your way up the road again and turn off along the path on the right shortly after the holiday centre buildings. The coastal path over the dunes will take you along beside the sea, but this is private estate so respect it accordingly. The path continues over the creek at Ti-Louzou (not labelled on map). Turn on to the road and then take the path on your right which leads to a house. When you have passed the stream (IGN ref 28), you should pick up the path again as it runs along beside the fields. Make your way along beneath the farm and then take the road leading to the marina at Térénez.

TÉRÉNEZ

Just before the port, the GR makes its way along a path known as rue de Paris (Paris Street). When you come to the road go along it and then turn along the path which climbs up to the right after the crossroads. Follow the road to the hamlet of Kerbahu, and then drop

95

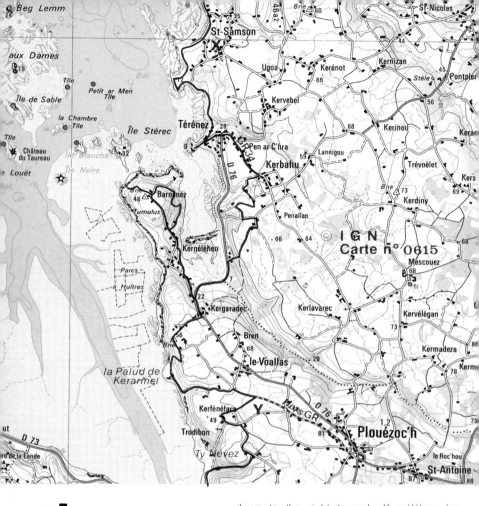

6Km
1:30

down to the right towards Kernéléhen (or Kernoanen). A left turn will take you across the farm and you should then make your way up the track leading to the estate. Turn first right and then left along a road. When you get to the bend, turn left and then right into a farmyard. Continue out across the fields, you will come to two paths. Take the one that drops down ahead of you. It bends to the right a little further on and drops quite steeply. You come out on the D76, where you should turn left and make your way round the bay. You will pass a campsite and come to a crossroads just north of Keragadec. Turn right towards Barnénez Tumulus (see left).

Barnénez Tumulus
3150 BC burial ground.
Enormous slabs protect
eleven dolmens. The
chamber is protected by a
mound of stones standing
1¹/₂ metres high. The site
almost disappeared under
the pickaxe and shovel of an
enthusiastic entrepreneur
who used it as a stone
quarry.

Detour
Viewpoint

4Km
1

Detour see left. If you follow the path which drops straight down to the beach, you will have a good view over Morlaix bay, with Sterec island, Taureau Château (Bull Château), Carantec and Callot island. Please respect the fences which have been put up. Efforts are being made to obtain permission for the GR to follow the coast right round the point. The marking will then change, of course.

When it gets to Barnénez (boundary stone), the GR heads right, along a path which drops down to Perrohen (not marked) and then follows a path on the right to the shore. You should turn right and make your way past the oyster beds below (dotted lines on map). At low tide, you can continue along the shore. At very high tides, make your way between the two hedges and over the estate. You should then take the lane between the oyster farm outbuildings and head south along the road. Take the D76 to Kergaradec, and turn right towards Kerberiou. Before you start to drop down, you should follow the cart track beside the grass. Pass the embankment then take the road which runs along the crest and then drop down to La Palud de Kerarmel.

La Palud de Kerarmel

Detour, *15 mins*
PLOUEZOC'H
⚒ 🚌
The 17th century church has
an interesting altar-piece,
statues, and a curious cross
called a 'hosanna' cross.

5Km
1:15

At low tide, you can get to Dourduff-en-Mer along the shore (the route is unmarked). The GR follows the road inland to a crossroads (see Y on the map).
     The GR then turns right along a lane to Datar Izella (not labelled on map). Make your way round Kerféneface farm and then turn left along the road, then right at the crossroads to Ty Nevez farm. Turn right after the farm, along the lane which leads to La Palud de Trodibon, and then follow the road to Le Dourduff-en-Mer.

Le Dourduff-en-Mer

3Km
0:45

PLOUJEAN

⚑ ✕ ⚏

11th–15th century church;
16th century bell-tower,
portal and charnel-house;
Gothic statue of the Virgin
Mary.

4Km
1

MORLAIX

ⓗ ⌂ ⚑ ✕ ♈
⚏ 🚋 🚌 🄕

The city is situated at the
confluence of the River Jarlat
and the River Queffleuth.
The port lies on the River
Morlaix.
Churches of Sainte-Melanie,
built in flamboyant Gothic
style; Saint-Mathieu (part
Renaissance);
Saint-Martin-des-Champs
(18th century); several old
houses; museum in the old
Dominican monastery; in the
town itself, there is the Les
Venelles pedestrian tour; the
railway line crosses over the
bottom of the town on an
enormous viaduct.

Turn right along the D76 and then left a few metres after the bridge, along a passage which runs along below the wood. As you approach the old transformer, turn right into the wood above the sunken track. After the wooden bridge, you should drop down to this track and then climb up opposite to the gardens at Suscinio (or Chuchuniou) Château. Climb up the steps and make your way round the château. You go along beside the chapel and take the exit from the gardens opposite the *conciergerie* (where the *concierge* or housekeeper lives). Turn left along the road at the first crossroads, then take the second left turn, carry straight on for about 1 kilometre, then turn left and then right to Ploujean.

The GR turns right along La Rue de La Maison de Paille (Straw House Street), and heads towards Roz ar Menez when it comes to the cross. You pass a farm, Keranroux Château (where you have right of way), and further on a dovecote before you pass between two enormous fountains. After the guardhouse, you come out on a road which takes you past a viaduct. Turn left along the road to Bas de la Rivière. Make your way round the harbour to Morlaix, where the walk comes to an end.

WALK 2

1Km
0:15

AVRANCHES

The town is situated on a hill at a height of 103 metres overlooking the Sée estuary and the whole Mont Saint-Michel bay. The raised terrace at Place Patton commemorates the decisive breakthrough at Avranches in 1944.

D104

This spot and the footbridge you've just crossed is one of the best for appreciating the force of the current at a spring tide. A wall of water, or bore, builds up and flows rapidly towards the head water where the sea and river meet. The bore arrives here 10 minutes before high tide.

8Km
2

The walk starts at the Jardin Public (Public Gardens) which overlook the whole bay of Mont Saint-Michel. From the south corner of the square, near the stone cross, the GR223 is signposted at the beginning of the Rue des Capucins and again at the gentle Gué de l'Epine hill. Turn right 100 metres further on into the Rue Jean-Nu-Pieds. Keep going down the hill for another 100 metres and then turn right again, heading west, into a small tarmac road which eventually becomes a steep path. This leads to the road (D104).

The GR223 follows the D104 to the right. It turns left 400 metres further on, over a footbridge which crosses the railway line and the river Sée. Continue along this road which leads to the D911. Fork gently left and you can walk along a grass track which runs parallel to the road (towards the south-west) and borders the river.

Continue along the path until you reach the hamlet of Le Rivage, then take the road across the stream and follow the grassy path. You will skirt the racecourse and several houses.

Shortly after the hamlet of La Vacquerie, leave the grassy path and take the paved track to your right. This becomes a road (D459) which you follow for 1.5 kilometres until you get to a bridge. Cross this and turn immediately left onto the grassy path opposite Gisors farm. If the going on the grassy path becomes difficult you can continue along the road (the route is marked). In this case, follow the road for another 800 metres and then turn left onto a road which takes you down to the shore. If the grassy path is passable, continue southwards alongside the fields. When you reach a fence, walk along beside the arm of the river which flows nearby and head in the same direction. You will come to a rocky headland facing south-east. Skirt the rocks and follow the river bed until you reach a second rocky headland facing south-west. Climb over the rocks out to the point called Le Grouin du Sud.

© **I G N**
Carte nº 1215

Grouin du Sud

From here, you have a view of the whole Mont Saint-Michel bay. The flowing water below is made up of the two rivers in the bay: the Sée and the Sélune. The characteristic sound of the bar can be heard an hour and a quarter before high tide.

5Km
1:30

Detour
Saint-Léonard

Ancient priory. 12th century church is the only remaining part.

GENÊTS

If you wish to cross the sandbanks towards Mont Saint-Michel, do not go alone. The tides, mists and quicksands can all be very dangerous. Seek advice from the guide.

5Km
1:15

La Dune
Detour, *20 mins*
DRAGEY

3Km
0:45

Rejoin the grassy path on the headland and take first the path heading north-north-west and then the paved track which leads to a road. Follow this for 1 kilometre to the farm Le Routout, situated on your left. Turn left here (west) and take the track which rejoins the grassy path. Follow the fencing in a north-north-west direction. You will come to a spot called La Chausée, which is on the site of the road formerly taken by Mont Saint-Michel pilgrims (where there is a statue of Saint-Léonard).

The GR follows the grassy path in a north-westerly direction and runs alongside gardens until it reaches a cluster of houses at Le Grand Port, a former fishing port. Take the same path to the farm Les Portaux, at the foot of the Manet hill. Take the road which runs away from the farm, but where it forks right continue straight on along a farm track, which may well be cultivated. This leads to Genêts.

Go through the market town of Genêts and turn left onto the D911. Follow this to the bridge crossing a little estuary and immediately afterwards head left (west) and skirt the grass for some 700 metres. Cross another small bridge and continue to Bec d'Andaine. You will come to the beach. Head right (east) along the shore to the car park which marks the end of the D35E. Cross the car park on the right hand side, and after about 300 metres turn left. Turn left again 400 metres further on and rejoin the shoreline which you should follow to the foot of the dunes (markings may be infrequent due to erosion from the sand). Continue to the D143, which leads to a beach overlooked by a few houses at La Dune.

Take the road on your right which passes through Potrel. At the crossroads at Launay turn right along the D143, which leads to the market town centre.

Continue along the shoreline for about 1 kilometre and turn right along a small path. You will cross another road and eventually arrive at the hamlet of Obrey (you may find accommodation at the farm). The road bends to the left and, 150 metres further on, take the first left which leads into Saint-Jean-le-Thomas.

SAINT-JEAN-LE-THOMAS
🏠 ⛺ ✕ ⚓ 🚌 🚲

Head right up the D911 for 300 metres. Take the small road on your left just before the cemetery and turn right along the D241. Follow this to a crossroads with a wayside cross and turn left again. The path wends its way into the woods above Saint-Jean-le-Thomas. After leaving the woods, you will come to a crossroads at La Gare.

LA GARE
🏠 ✕

Take the D911 towards Granville for about 400 metres, and then head left on a path that crosses the fields and drops down into a wood. You will come out onto another path, which you follow. It bends right along the cliff towards a lane which will lead you back to the D911. Go left along the D911 for about 200 metres, and then take a track on your left leading to a little stone hut. The coastguard path starts behind this hut, and you should follow it along the clifftop for a few kilometres until you come to another stone hut, Cabane Vauban.

6Km
1:30

Cabane Vauban
Detour, *30 mins*
CAROLLES
🏠 ⛺ ✕ ⚓ 🚌
(See dotted line on map.)

After leaving the hut at Cabane Vauban, turn sharp right 400 metres later onto a small path, and after a few metres drop down a steep slope to the left until you get to the Lude stream. Go over the little bridge and then turn right. This road will take you to the outskirts of Carolles. The old railway track will lead you to the main road at Carolles.

From the hut at Cabane Vauban, the GR223 follows the cliffs to the Lude harbour (not labelled). Crcoss the Lude stream and then follow its course for 100 metres before taking the path on the left which winds its way to the top of the cliff (if you follow the stream down the valley you will also get to Carolles).

3Km
1

Continue along the cliff until you reach a panoramic viewpoint with a map of the surrounding area. Climb just a little further to the right and cross the car park. The GR is now on your left, where it skirts the neighbouring houses. It then drops down to the road coming from Plage de Edenville (not labelled on map).

Plage de Edenville
🏠 ✕ ⚓

As you arrive at this road, turn right and cross the D911 to a path which runs alongside the Crapeux stream through Vallée des Peintres (Artists' Valley). After about 300 metres, follow

13Km
3:30

SAINT-PAIR-SUR-MER
⌂ ⋏

GRANVILLE

Old quarter; ramparts;
Pointe du Roc on the
2Km   *headland.*
0:30

Base d'Hélicoptères

the disused railway platform and cross the viaduct to another road. Skirt the foot of a steep cliff on your left, continue for 200 metres and then climb the steps between the houses. These are almost hidden, but look for the wicket gate. You will then reach a path on top of the cliff. Follow it to the left for about 400 metres, turn right and then shortly afterwards left onto a road which leads to Bouillon, where camping sites are available (see map). Country lanes will take you to the hamlets of Carrière and Lézeaux. The D21 will take you across the Thar river, and 500 metres further on you should turn sharp left (west). Follow the little road, which meanders along between the hedgerows, until you reach a well. Carry on for another 250 metres then turn left. After a further 500 metres, turn right. You can look down on the hamlet of Kairon. Shortly afterwards you cross two roads and then, further on, the D373. Go straight on to Catteville. There, take the D569 to the right, to Trois-Croix, then turn left onto the D21 towards Saint-Pair. If you want to skirt Saint-Pair-sur-Mer, take the second road on the right after Trois-Croix.

Continue along wide paths and roads among the houses which take you through the outskirts of the town. Cross the River Saigne, cut across the D135 and another major road and you will arrive eventually at the high school in Granville.

The GR passes in front of the station at Granville, follows the Rue de la Gare for 500 metres and heads off left down some steps to cross the Granville-Coutances road (D971).

The GR then leaves the town at the Pointe du Lude, that rears up behind the beach at Donville-les-Bains. From the point, go down to the beach and follow the route along the shore towards the Base d'Hélicoptères (helicopter base).

As the GR runs alongside defence territory at this point, you may find you are forbidden access when shooting practice is in progress. You can miss out this point of the route by following the directions below, which will take you off the GR.

4Km
1

16Km
4

Alternative (inland) route from the Base d'Hélicoptères to Coudeville-Plage. At the helicopter base, take the road on your right which leads to a quarry. Climb up to the small village of La Bergerie and head for the parish church. Take the road to Bréville and then wend your way through the various little villages until you rejoin the GR near Coudeville-Plage. (See dotted line on the map.)

The GR continues along behind the race-course, along the shore or among the sand dunes. You skirt the firing range and come to the beach at Coudeville – Saint-Martin-de-Bréhal.

COUDEVILLE-PLAGE-SAINT-MARTIN-DE-BREHAL
◯ Å ✕ ⌑

This part of the Channel coastline is characterised by harbours such as La Vanlée, Régneville and La Sienne which are estuaries where the sea flows in at high tide.

Here you will see so-called mielles, *which is sandy agricultural land. Here farmers grow carrots enriched by seaweed and kelp, and well known for their tenderness.*

As you come into Coudeville-Plage, turn right onto the D351. After 800 metres, take the road on your left which will lead to the D592. Take this eastwards for 200 metres. Now turn left (north) for several kilometres, skirting the Havre de la Vanlée (salt flats, which are covered with water at high tide).

Continue along keeping the harbour on your right. You will come to a campsite on your left. The GR will veer off to the right and then right again at the beginning of a road which may well be flooded. Take this so-called *Route Submersible* and head east across the harbour.

Turn left onto a road which meanders along between the houses of Les Salines (so-called because of the salt works). Keep an eye out for signposts, as the GR winds in and out of the fields.

Take the D278 right and then the D298, to the little village of La Planche Guillemette, then turn left (west) back towards the sea. Turn right (north) at Les Hardes and follow the route to Le Pont Brun, where you turn right onto the D220 (east). After 300 metres, turn left and you will come to another road which you should follow in a westerly direction. Just before you reach the shoreline, turn right (north) onto a small track which crosses the sand dunes and takes you to the beach at Hauteville-sur-Mer.

5Km
1:15

5Km
1:15

7Km
1:45

Hauteville-sur-Mer

MONTMARTIN-SUR-MER

LE PONT DE LA ROQUE

When you reach the outskirts of Hauteville-sur-Mer, turn right and then left just before the canal bridge. Turn left again onto the D356 and then a little further on, head right (north) along a path which joins up with the D76. Again you should head right on the D76 until you come to a canal bridge. Turn to the left here (north), until you reach a road which you should follow eastwards to the hamlet of Ourville. Continue north-east across the meadows to Montmartin-sur-Mer.

Leave the town on the D73 going west towards the sea. When you reach the houses a little further on, take the road on your right going north. Head left on the D249 for a few metres and then turn right (north) along a path which runs across some old quarries towards the little village of La Rousserie a few kilometres further on. Here, the GR turns right (east) and, 500 metres further on, right again on to the D156. You should then turn left along the D20 until you reach Le Pont de la Roque.

Here, the GR goes inland for some considerable distance. When you have passed the two bridges, follow the Coutances road (D20) for 1.2 kilometres to the village of Le Coisel. On leaving the village, turn left until you reach the farm Le Blondel. Take the sunken road on your right. Further on, take the road on the right which climbs towards the market town of Bricqueville-la-Blouette. Head immediately left, and take the road which drops down north towards the stream. Before you reach this turn off on the road on your right, to the little village of Le Bois. Continue along the dirt track which starts opposite the outlying houses at the other end of the village. Turn right 500 metres further on, and pass underneath an overhead electric cable. Not long after this, you should take the private road leading to the agricultural college in Coutances, and leave the water tower behind on your left. Stay on the private road across the college grounds. When you reach the buildings, head left along a path shaded by beech trees. You will pass a pond, where you turn right 200 metres later along a path which drops down into a wood and takes you to the outskirts of the hamlet of Turpin (not labelled on map). The street on the right will take you to Coutances.

COUTANCES

Cathedral (11th and 13th centuries), with two towers crowned with tall narrow spires (77 metres), façade decorated with wrought-iron work of the galerie des roses (rose gallery), and an octagonal lantern-turret (57 metres high); local people call this turret the plomb; churches of Saint-Pierre and Saint-Nicholas (15th and 16th centuries); gardens open to the public; museum.

6Km
1:30

Note: *The roads between Coutances and Lessay are often very muddy in Winter and Spring.*

MONTHUCHON

6Km
1:30

Drop down the Rue des Piliers towards Coutainville and cross over the D44. Continue for 80 metres and then head right on a small path which runs alongside the 15th century aquaduct and then turns left and skirts the cemetery. Cut across another road and turn right onto the D293. Cross the D2 and continue for 1.3 kilometres. Take the little road on your right, which takes you to a group of houses where you turn left onto a road which runs for 1.2 kilometres to the hamlet of La Michellière. Continue in a straight line to the D57 where you turn right and head for Monthuchon.

Turn left as you enter the village and take the path heading west-north-west which leads to the hamlets of La Guérie-de-Bas and Les Vaux. It meets up with another road where you should turn left. Continue for 250 metres until you turn right (north) towards the village of La Petite Délairie. Here a little road heading due north will take you to a cluster of houses called L'Hôtel-Joie (not labelled on map). Turn left in front of these houses and right 250 metres later. When you come to a bend in the road turn left (west). Continue for 1.6 kilometres until you reach a little road on your right which will lead you to the hamlet of Le Pont (not labelled) and then on to the village of Ancteville.

ANCTEVILLE
⌂

4Km
1

Head left out of the village past the cross. Turn right (north) and continue along a wide path until you reach a group of buildings. Turn right here (east) onto the D436 and shortly afterwards left past the Grand Moulin (fish farm). You reach a bend in the road 500 metres later, turn off to the left and, when you reach the D53, cut straight across it. After 600 metres turn left to Muneville-le-Bingard.

MUNEVILLE-LE-BINGARD
✖ ♈ ⚖

8Km
2

Leave the village on the D53 (west) and head right after the cross to join up with the D68. Turn right and follow this road for about 100 metres, and then take the road which leads to the hamlet of Coquière. There, take the path which bends left and then right, and takes you to the hamlet of Haut-du-Bingard. When you reach the D434, turn right and then immediately left (north). Drop down a path to a little road, then head left (west), cross the D2 and continue on the same road for about 1 kilometre. After a muddy bit of track, turn left and cross the D53 towards the Les Oies Landes. (You can camp or bivouac at the farm and also purchase farm produce.) Continue to the market town of Gefosses.

GEFOSSES
⚠ ✖ ♈ ⚖

7Km
1:45

Pass the church and take the D53 towards the sea in a westerly direction. Turn right after 200 metres and left further on. You will cut across the D72 and then a smaller road (D531). Go through the hamlet of La Maresquière and then cross the Douit stream. You will come to the D432 and should turn left to La Morinière. Here, take the road on your right (north), and after a turning in the road, take the road heading towards La Carbonnellerie. On leaving the hamlet, you will cross a stream and cut across a road. The GR will then turn first left (west) and then right (north). Look out for the 11th and 12th century Château de Pirou on your right. Turn right at the road, and go through the hamlet of La Bosquerie. You will then cross the D94. Bend gently right and take the path leading to the village of Pirou-le-Pont (Le Pont on map).

Pirou-le-Pont

When the weather is wet, continue straight on after the bridge and take the second road on your right (see dotted line on map) which leads to Les Croûtes.

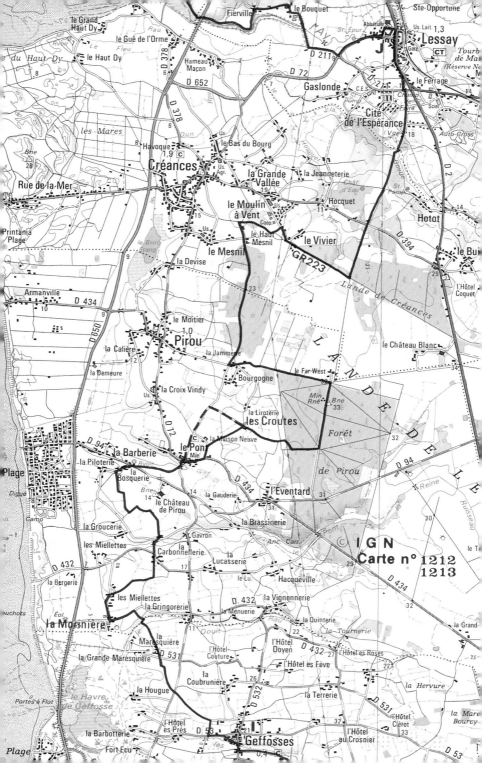

3Km
0:45

Le Far West

8Km
2

After the bridge, the GR turns right. Pass the town hall and turn left (north) 300 metres later along a lane bordered with hedgerows. When you reach Les Croûtes turn right (east) opposite a large shed, and the road will plunge you into the depths of the Pirou forest. In the forest, you will come to a tarmac lane, and you turn left along this, heading north. You will pass the ruins of an old mill, and as you emerge from the forest you will come across a cluster of houses at Le Far West

At the end of the road, the GR bends left towards the village of Bourgogne. Turn right at the last house. The road plunges again into the forest (take care to follow the signs) and continues almost continuously in the same direction, due north. When you leave the forest, go through the hamlet of Le Haut-Mesnil and then take the first track on your right to Le Vivier. Follow this and take the wide road opposite at Le Vivier. After about 1 kilometre turn left (north) through the woods. Cut across the D394 and, after about 1 kilometre, cross a small bridge and turn left. You will come out onto the fairground. Cross this and the pavement straight ahead of you will lead to Lessay's abbey church.

LESSAY

The Sainte-Croix fair takes place on the weekend closest to 11/12th September. It has been a popular event since the Middle Ages. 11th century abbey church with high nave with seven bays; carefully restored after being damaged in 1944. There are many footpaths and walks in the area.

6Km
1:30

From the south portal of the abbey church, take the road bordered by lime trees and turn right at the end. At the first crossroads 1 kilometre later, turn right again. When you reach Havre de Lessay, turn right onto an embankment to cross the River Ay (make sure you shut the gate, as this part of the route takes you across private land). After a stone bridge, the GR passes between large sheds, takes a private road on the right and then turns left. After 500 metres, when you get to Fierville, head left and walk along beside the River Ay. You will cross the holiday route (D650).

Continue along the edge of Havre de Lessay and you will reach the road leading to the market town of Saint-Germain-sur-Ay.

SAINT-GERMAIN-SUR-AY

6Km
1:30

Cross the town, turn left in front of the church, and rejoin Lessay harbour. Head right and follow the grassy path until you come to an ancient guard-house Le Corps de Garde, Cabane Vauban (Vauban hut), called chapelle (the chapel). Turn right and head for the D306 at the hamlet of La Gaverie. Follow this road left and cross a strip of water. After you have passed the road (D527) to Bretteville, head right to the second sandy track, which is bordered by fir trees. This track meanders along until it reaches a road, and here you should turn first right and then left. The GR heads towards the sea, passes various villas and leaves Saint-Germain-sur-Ay-Plage on its left (south) as it bends right (north-west) and passes through the fir trees. Follow the small road behind the sand dunes until you reach a wooden chalet. Go through the gate, making sure that you shut it behind you. After 1 kilometre you will come to La Plage at Bretteville-sur-Ay (see K on map).

Plage de Bretteville-sur-Ay

6Km
1:30

From La Plage the GR follows the shore, sometimes wending its way through the sand dunes and sometimes along the beach itself when it comes up against barbed wire. You will eventually come to the D526 at the cluster of houses at La Poudrière, where you turn right and head towards the church at Surville.

Eglise de Surville

Turn left (north) just before the church and follow the *route touristique* (holiday route) for

6Km
1:30

5Km
1:15

8Km
2

DENNEVILLE-PLAGE

PORTBAIL

Notre-Dame is an ancient Norman sanctuary (11th and 12th centuries), with a magnificent 15th century fortified tower; remains of a Gallo-Roman font (discovered 1956) where baptism would have been by complete immersion. This must have been built at the end of the Dark Ages or the beginning of the Middle Ages, and is the only one of its type north of the Loire.

300 metres. Turn left at the end of the slip road and follow the path which runs alongside the harbour for 800 metres before you climb up an embankment on your left. Continue along beside the fencing until you come to an electricity plant in the middle of the fields, the so-called Mielles d'Allonne. (You will find markings rather far apart along this part of the route, as there are no supports.) Cross the road (D327) and continue north until you reach Denneville-Plage.

The GR goes through Denneville-Plage along the Rue A. Pelca and the Rue Charles Lefèbvre, which run beside the sea. After passing an embankment, you will run alongside a barbed wire fence. Turn right at the first house you come to at Lindbergh-Plage. Stay on this road for 100 metres and then head off down the grassy path. Turn right (east) along the winding track and then take the wide path opposite. You should then turn left along a track which will lead you to the D72E. Turn right (east) at the first house on your left and follow the sandy path. After a small quarry, you should head right along the path which runs parallel to the stream. At Havre de Portbail, turn right, go over the concrete footbridge across the estuary and follow the path on your left beside the harbour until you come to the church at Portbail.

From the church, the GR follows the D15 across Havre de Portbail. It turns right at the first houses on the beach and heads towards a riding stables (Centre Equestre) on a road that becomes narrower near the water tower. It then comes to a crossroads. There, the GR turns right and then left 600 metres later. It continues along through the fields, cuts across a small road and turns right after 100 metres. You should follow the small road for 400 metres and turn left onto a 4 kilometre stretch of track which goes straight across the fields (Les Mielles). You will cut across the D324, the D132 and then a path which heads right in the direction of Saint-Jean-la-Rivière before coming to the D166 and the Pré-Normand camping site on your left. Continue straight until you reach the south-east corner of Barneville-Carteret harbour and skirt it on the right-hand side to the D130.

© I G N
Carte n° 1211

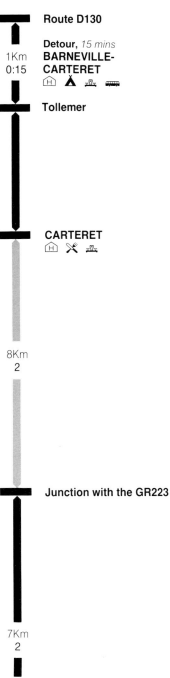

Route D130

Take the D130 right (north-east).

Detour, *15 mins*
1Km **BARNEVILLE-**
0:15 **CARTERET**

The GR crosses the D130 to the harbour's edge. Cross the estuary of the Le Tot stream and you will come to the hamlet of Tollemer.

Tollemer

From this hamlet, which lies just east of Carteret, you have a choice of three different routes: 1) Take the optional route from Carteret to Hatainville (yellow and red markings) (described below, see dotted line on map), 2) continue along the GR223 towards Les Moitiers d'Allonne, 3) go to the junction with the D902 and make for the gîte which is 800 metres on your right.

CARTERET

Alternative route from Carteret to Hatainville
At Tollemer, head left alongside Carteret harbour and go down the street La rue de Paris. At the ferry car park, turn first right and then left and climb up to the coast road. Follow this, and after a while, head left along the path which leads to the point at Cap de Carteret. At the other side of the point, you come to the ruins of an old church. Here, take the road again and a little higher up, turn left along a track which leads to a conifer plantation. Skirt this on the right-hand side. This area belongs to the *Conservatoire du Littoral* (Coastline Protection Body). You must take care as the ground is crumbly. Follow the fence north for 2.5 kilometres and go into the centre of Hatainville. Follow the D201 left to the cross and take the road opposite which joins up again with the GR223.

8Km
2

Junction with the GR223

At the hamlet of Tollemer, the GR223 heads right on the D902, crosses the railway line and turns immediately left. It runs alongside the track for about 200 metres. You then turn right and climb towards the hamlet of Quinetot. Cut across the D904 and climb gently uphill east and then north. Cross the D903 and then turn right and drop down towards a stream. Ford it, and then a few metres further on head left along the climbing zig-zag road. Turn left onto the D323 for a short distance and climb up the incline on your right towards the old windmills (you have a view across the whole area from here). Drop down again and head right along the D323. At the first junction, take the road

7Km
2

towards Le Bosquet and when you reach the little village, head right along the D425 to Néel. Go through it, then cross a stream a little further on. Take the unmade road until you come to a stone cross. Continue to Les Moitiers d'Allonne.

LES MOITIERS D'ALLONNE
⌂ ⟁ ♨

1.5Km
0:20

Take the D323 left beside the church which quickly cuts across the D904. Head right after 500 metres and turn immediately left onto the unmade road. This intersects with the D242 on the outskirts of Hatainville. At the second junction, you will join up with the Carteret-Hatainville route.

Junction with alternative route from Carteret to Hatainville

The GR continues west before taking a sharp right turn to the north.

8Km
2

From here, you can look across the dunes, which are like real mountains hewn out of sand and are some of the highest on the Normandy coastline. The view stretches beyond the Cap du Rozel to the Cap de Flamanville and the Pieux hill (Hill of the Faithful).

For the next 5 kilometres the GR follows a tarmac road which runs almost in a straight line. You will come across few people as you walk along between the wide grassy banks on each side, crossing the D131 and passing through a few small hamlets, to Surtainville.

SURTAINVILLE
⌂ ▲ ✕ ♨

Shortly after the church at Surtainville, the GR turns left and passes through Le Bas-Hamel. When you reach Les Focs, turn left and take the D66 for 750 metres. Turn right towards Les Sablières. When you reach the top of the campsite, continue straight on. The GR223 runs along a private road (camping is strictly forbidden here, and make sure you keep to the path) and turns right. When you reach the hamlet of Le Pou, head left on the D517 and then turn left again down Trompe-Souris street which leads to the sea. Climb up some steps to an old blockhouse. The GR climbs up the cliff and follows the coastline past Cap du Rozel. You will pass close by the statue of Maris Stella and then begin to drop down to Le Ranch campsite. Skirt this and then turn first right and then left along an unmade road. When you reach the stream, head right and then shortly afterwards left through the village of Le Rozel.

8Km
2

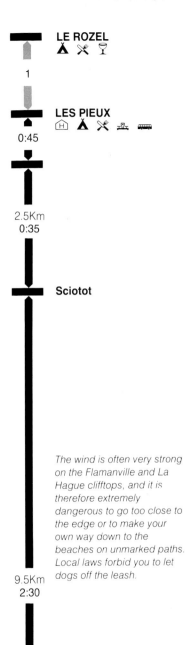

LE ROZEL

LES PIEUX
0:45

2.5Km
0:35

Sciotot

The wind is often very strong on the Flamanville and La Hague clifftops, and it is therefore extremely dangerous to go too close to the edge or to make your own way down to the beaches on unmarked paths. Local laws forbid you to let dogs off the leash.

9.5Km
2:30

Detour
FLAMANVILLE

When you reach Moitié,

Alternative route from Le Rozel to Sciotot. As you leave Le Rozel, you can take an alternative route, marked in yellow and red, which passes through the Hochet valley and leads to Les Pieux.

Cross the Pieux heath after leaving the town and you will rejoin the GR at Sciotot. (See dotted line on the map.)

The GR passes in front of Le Rozel chateau, and turns left off the D517 to L'Ecluse. You should head right until you reach another road and then follow this left. Just before you reach the Grand Large campsite, turn right and then left. The GR joins up with the D517 when it reaches the hamlet of L'Hôtel Saint-Vast, and then heads left along the road to the village of Sciotot.

Here you meet up with the alternative route coming from Les Pieux, marked in yellow and red. Continue along the D517. When you reach the hamlet of Courtois, head off on the road on the left and you will join up with the coast at Le Fortin (not labelled on map). Follow the stone embankment until you reach the site of the old road which was destroyed by the sea. You rejoin the D517 at this point and you should head left along it. Then take the track on the left which leads to a stone quarry, which you go across. The GR now follows the cliff.

Turn right at the first crossroads, and then left after 50 metres. Take the path on your left 500 metres later, which drops down towards the west. Shortly afterwards leave this path and climb up the cliff, you will come out on the signal-station road. Follow a low stone wall and then turn immediately left. At the first track you come to which is suitable for motor vehicles, turn left and head downhill for about 50 metres before bending right. The coastal path comes to an end at Anse de Quédoy, at the electro-nuclear power station fence. Here the GR heads straight on towards the hamlet of Moitié (not labelled on map).

127

*continue straight on for 400
metres. Church (1670),
paved with flat stones, each
with a haloed cross; château,
a rather ramshackle
grey-stone building (17th
and 18th centuries),
surrounded by ornamental
lakes.*

From Moitié the GR heads left through the old hamlets of La Coquaise, Courtois, Les Louis and La Botterie with their stone houses.

*After La Berquerie, you can
look down on the valley
housing the old underwater
iron works, closed in 1962.*

After La Berquerie (not labelled on map), turn right along an earth track, head downhill and cross the road, then climb up towards the cliff at Le Bec (not labelled on map). The GR cuts across two more roads and then drops steeply down towards Diélette, giving you a good view of this village and of Siouville and Vauville bay.

DIÉLETTE
⌂ Λ ✕ ⚎

After the port at Diélette, take the D4 north. When you come to the top of the old quarry, situated just after the ramp leading to the beach, take the coastal footpath on your left which cuts across private land and looks down on the beach at Le Platé. This heads towards Saint-Pierre hill and you should skirt the hill back towards the D4. Climb up to the hamlet of Sauvage, where you should turn left and bend almost immediately right along a small path which wends its way up to the church at Siouville.

4Km
1

SIOUVILLE
⌂ ⌂ Λ ✕ ⚎

Take the D64 left for 100 metres, and head off on the wide track on your left. You cross the D64 at La Viéville, and then shortly afterwards cross the road leading to the hamlet of Es Francs. Turn left at the next path and then right shortly afterwards along a sunken track. This comes out at Pont-Langlois, which you should cross before turning immediately left. Cross the second stream you come to, and then climb up to the right. You will cut across one track and should then turn left at the second, 400 metres later. You will find yourself dropping down to dunes which are used as a military firing range. From here right up to south of Vauville, the GR runs alongside defence territory which is indicated from time to time.

Important! As the zone is dangerous, it is forbidden to walk along the GR while firing exercises are taking place. There are no

9Km
2:30

© IGN
Carte n° 1110 1210

exercises in July and August, but at other times of the year, you should make enquiries at the town halls in Siouville, Vasteville or Biville, or at the police station in Beaumont-Hague. As you approach the firing range, turn sharp right and follow the fence running alongside the outlying fields until you come to a paved track. You will leave the Pénitot road and then the D123 at Le Pont des Sablons behind on your right. Shortly afterwards, ford the Les Sablons stream and on the other side take the paved track to the D37. Follow this for a few metres and turn left along the first path which runs beside a stream. Cross this and then turn right. If the ground is soggy, take the embankment. You will come to a paved path and you should take this left. You will climb up to a small road which you should follow to' Biville.

BIVILLE
⌂ ⌾

Church, with a 13th century choir and 16th century bas-reliefs, contains relics of Thomas the Blessed, chaplain of Saint Louis.

6Km
1:30

The GR doesn't actually go into the village. When it reaches the hamlet of Gardin, it takes a sharp left to take the coast road which looks down on the Gardin valley. It then heads north and leads to the Calvaire des Dunes (Cross in the Dunes).

The traveller now enters a land of dunes, some of which may at times be more than 100 metres high. Their plants, flowers and insects make the dunes a living area. For this reason, ramblers are requested to show respect for nature when they pass through, and are asked not to pick plants or grass or to set up camp.

Pass behind the Calvaire des Dunes. The GR runs first of all alongside the fence surrounding the outlying fields and then takes a sharp turn towards the sea. It follows the north side of a long dune which marks the limits of the Val Tollé on its right edge. Drop down and bend right, and then cross the stream which has high banks on each side. You will come to a large sand quarry. From there, take a paved track to the D237 and follow this to the hamlet of Le Petit Thot. You should then take the first road on your right and shortly afterwards, turn right again along a path which climbs the hill. You will pass close to the fountain of Thomas the Blessed, which stands opposite some ruins. Once at the top of the hill, drop down to the D318 and follow it left to Vauville.

© I G N
Carte n° 1110

VAUVILLE
⚑ ⛲

Priory and church (12th and the 15th centuries, respectively).

From Vauville, the GR follows the Cap de la Hague cliffs for 15 kilometres along coastguard paths until it finally comes to the port of Goury. The GR winds its way along the top of the shale and sandstone cliffs which are between 50 and 110 metres high. Watch out for strong winds all along this part of the route.

Detour in the area surrounding Vauville, there are three interesting unmarked walks: 1) via the heaths of Catillon, 2) via the stones of Pouquelées, 3) via Les Treize Vents (the thirteen winds). (See dotted line on the map.)

6Km 1:45

From here, you can look out over the coves, which are like creeks or beaches hemmed in by rocks, and also over the Nez de Jobourg and Nez de Voidries. This is one of the most beautiful parts of the Cotentin route.

Important! It is extremely dangerous to try and get down onto the beaches from the cliffs or to venture off marked paths.

The GR crosses Vauville via the D318 and you should leave the road and head left at the cluster of houses at La Grecque. Follow a path which overlooks the sea as it meanders between low stone walls and pass through the old village of Le Petit Beaumont (not labelled on map). You will come to the car park which is situated on the hill down to Herquemoulin on the D403 and you should follow this road left. Turn left 400 metres later, along a track which heads towards the sea: you will come across clumps of tamarisk every now and then at the roadside. Cross a stream and walk along a stone wall. Be careful to watch out for markings. The footpath runs along Fontanelles bay. When you get to the end, go down the steps to Anse des Moulinets.

Anse des Moulinets

Above you, you can see the entertainment suites belonging to the Atomic Energy Centre (CEA), which are closed to the public. You can also see the dam built by the CEA to cater for its factory's water needs.

5Km 1:30

Cross the dam overflow on a footbridge and then climb onto the other bank. When you get to the corner of the fence at the top, head straight on. The GR cuts across the Margot valley over a little stream and then continues afterwards along the clifftops. It zigzags down the slope La Gravelette (at Pointe à L'Eau Goulex), and you should be careful not to go right by mistake towards the village of Dannery. After the Montcanval valley, the GR heads off once again along a rocky spur. Make sure you don't take the track which drops down to Anse de Pivette (Pivette Cove). Climb sharply to the right to get round the cove and you will reach the Nez de Jobourg (nature reserve for birds). The GR leads on to the Nez de Voidries.

133

NEZ DE VOIDRIES

5Km
1:30

La Roche

1Km
0:15

GOURY

A stone cross was erected in memory of the submarine Le Vendémiaire which went down with all its crew during manoeuvres in 1912.

Detour, *15 mins*
AUDERVILLE

6.5Km
1:30

PORT RACINE

This is the smallest port in France within the jurisdiction of Saint-Germain-des-Vaux. Jacques Prévert gardens, situated nearby in the Moulins valley, are open to the public.

6.5Km
1:45

OMONVILLE-LA-ROGUE

From the old signal tower, the GR drops down to Anse du Culeron (Culeron Cove), towards Baie d'Ecalgrain. It rejoins the D401 and follows it left. When you get almost to the top of the slope, take the path on your left which you will find meanders along beside the sea to the village of La Roche.

Detour A circular unmarked route leaves the village and meanders through Merquetot and Laye before joining up with the GR at the Moulin (mill) stream. (See dotted line on the map.)

The GR will lead you to the little port of Goury.

From the tip of La Hague, the GR follows the coastal path and then takes the D401 around the La Hague signal tower. Continue in the same direction and you will reach the Roche Gélétan at the end of the D402. Excavations here have uncovered signs of habitation some 200,000 years old. Continue along the coastal path without turning off along the roads to the right. Further on, after passing the D202, head right along the D45 which overlooks Port Racine.

Continue along the D45 to the Pointe du Nez, drop down a few steps to the beach and skirt Anse Saint-Martin (Saint Martin's Cove) on the coastal path. After 2 or 3 kilometres, after the Baie d'Ecuty, pass the signal tower on Pointe Jardeheu. Follow the shingle bank and you will come to the jetty at Omonville-la-Rogue.

Detours You can take two circular routes from Omonville-la-Rogue, each approximately 10 kilometres long: 1) From Omonville via Vallace valley, Croix du bon repos, Grand Bel farm, the hamlet of La Fosse and then Es-Fours, after which you rejoin the GR, further back at

© **I G N**
Carte n° 1110 1210

8Km
2:30

The fortress houses the curious Muraille de Chine (Great Wall of China), a panorama of the stretch from Cherbourg to Cap de Fermanville.

LANDEMER
🏠 ✕

the D245. 2) From Omonville via Manoir (manor house) du Tourp, the church at d'Eculleville and the Sabine valley, returning via the GR along the coast. (See dotted lines on the map.)

At the first house after Omonville port the GR turns left. It leads along a path to the old fortress.

The GR continues along the cliff path. It skirts Baie des Fontenelles, passes the Cotentine farm ruins, and leads to Baie de la Quervière car park at the end of the D402. Shortly after crossing a stream, it meanders along close to the Mur Blanc, which is a point of reference for those at sea. About 2 kilometres further on, just before you reach the rocks at Castel Vendon, you can climb up a path to Hameau Gruchy (Gréville-Hague), where the artist Jean-François Millet was born. The GR now comes to Landemer.

Just after the intersection with the D45, you drop down left towards the sea and set off again along the coastal path. This runs alongside fields which are occasionally subject to erosion from the sea.

1.5Km
0:30

You can see the Mur de l'Atlantique (Atlantic Wall) blockhouses from the 1939–1945 war which stand precariously on the shore.

URVILLE-NACQUEVILLE

4Km
1

QUERCQUEVILLE

Detour,
CHERBOURG

The area of Nord Cotentin around Cherbourg is the only part of the region that is really industrialised: there are shipyards, mechanical and electrical firms, a factory dealing with the re-cycling of atomic waste (La Hague), and a nuclear power station (Flamanville). Military activity in Cherbourg port has considerably reduced, and the town now has an important fishing industry.

The passenger port with its fleet of car ferries is also very active. The marina accommodates more than 5000 boats each year. Roule fortress; the War and Liberation Museum; the Museum of Fine Arts.

Head along several streets running parallel to the sea near the beach at Urville-Nacqueville.

The coastal path continues east along the beach. It passes the old fortress at Nacqueville and the cluster of houses at La Rue du Nez. Head along the beach at Anse de Quercqueville until you reach the private campsite belonging to the navy. Turn right and follow the fences surrounding the naval instruction centre until you get to the D45 at Quercqueville.

Signposts for the GR223 come to a stop here, as you are now in the suburbs of Cherbourg. (Buses for the centre leave half-hourly on weekdays from the railway station here.)

Signposts for the GR start again just before the town hall at Tourlaville.

TOURLAVILLE
ⓗ ◻ ✕ ⚒ 🚌

From Tourlaville, walkers have a choice between two different routes: 1) an alternative route, which goes via Tourlaville château, 2) the GR223 proper.

Alternative route via Tourlaville Château. Set off from the D901 opposite Tourlaville town hall (X on map). Climb up towards the church and take first the Rue de Verdun left, and then La Vieille Rue Sous la Rocade to the Les Flottes (the fleets) quarter. Then turn along the dirt track heading due south, which will lead to the D322 near Tourlaville Château.

**6Km
1:30**

The château is surrounded by moats and ponds, and is a beautiful example of Renaissance architecture. There is a museum open to the public containing a large collection of 17th and 18th century ceramics, together with weapons, suits of armour, tapestries, furniture and sculptures.

Take the D322 and go south round the château. At about 100 metres before you reach the hamlet of Saint-Jean, where bed and breakfast is available, take the dirt track on your left. You will pass a chapel and then a cross. Turn left, and then shortly afterwards right to the hamlet of Groult (not labelled on map), where you will intersect with the D63. Wide dirt tracks will take you to a road which you should cross at the hamlet of La Croix Perrinot. The route continues north, crosses the D120 and arrives at the chapel at the Carrefour de la Bonne Vierge Simonet (crossroads of Simonet, the Good Virgin), where it rejoins the GR223.

Carrefour de la Bonne Vierge Simonet

**3Km
0:45**

The GR223 leaves on the D901 just before Tourlaville town hall (X on map). It first heads left, turns right into the Rue Fournel, and then right again into the Rue Saint-Maur which eventually turns into a dirt track. You turn left back into Rue Fournal and head right to cut across the D120. A dirt track will take you to the D901 and you should cross this to the chapel at the Carrefour de la Bonne Vierge Simonet.

Carrefour de la Bonne Vierge Simonet

Detour If you follow the D320 north for 400 metres, you will find a shady path which runs alongside the road. This has been classified a megalithic conservation area.

Here you join up with the alternative route that went via Tourlaville château. The GR continues eastwards. It intersects with the D122, the D901 and then the D320.

141

© I G N
Carte n° 1210 1310

The GR continues east until it comes to a crossroads. Take the dirt track opposite and then left which runs alongside a series of ruins. Turn left along the road and then right at the chapel. Head left on the D611 for 500 metres and then take the short cut on your left which later joins up with the road again. Go right and then left to the hamlet of La Rue de Maupertus.

8Km
2

From here, you have a good view of the Nord Cotentin coast. You should be able to make out the artificial channels at the port of Cherbourg with their shipping passages. If you look east, you can see Cap Lévi with the outline of its modern lighthouse which shines out over Cherbourg channel.

You then pass through the market town of La Place and drop down to Anse du Brick.

ANSE DU BRICK

Cross the D116, drop down towards the beach and cross the stream on a footbridge. From here for the next 6 kilometres to the beach at Mondrée, the GR223 follows the sea along the coastal footpath. After about 3 metres this path enters private property, and you should therefore stay close to the sea and take the coast footpath that runs alongside the fences belonging to the different properties. You will pass the Pointe du Brûlé. Follow the track alongside Anse du Pied Sablon and then take the path leading to Port du Cap Lévi.

6Km
1:30

This little port goes back to Roman times. The jetties are built of pink stone which comes from the famous quarries near Fermanville.

Head left and skirt the west side of the old fortress. You should cross its courtyard (private property) by walking alongside the fence until you reach the stile. Cross this. You will come to Phare du Cap Lévi (lighthouse). Make your way round Cap Lévi. Continue past the quarry and Pignot Harbour (not labelled on map) and after several hundred metres, you will come to a cluster of houses at Castel de la Mondrée.

Castel de la Mondrée

You can set off from this point on a walk along the Val de Saire. The GR223 runs along Mondrée beach below the level of the dunes and at the eastern end heads across private land (use the stile rather than the gate). Turn left as you leave the beach.

At the western tip, Cap Lévi, archeologists found the remains of a prehistoric

© I G N
Carte n° 1210 1310

dwelling place dating from the Paleolithic Age. They dug down 18 metres beneath the surface, the only excavations of such depth in France.

Beneath the stone stele at the eastern tip of Cap Lévi are the remains of a 7th century boat uncovered by the seat.

This path continues all the way along the flat north-east Cotentin coast, and the marshes running alongside often extend to the sea. These were sometimes used to steep flax in byegone days, or to grow reeds for the thatched roofs on the cottages. The tracks beside the sea are often eaten away by winter storms. Situated between two strong currents (at Cap Lévi and Cap de Barfleur) which can be particularly fierce close to dry land, it is an inhospitable coastline for sailors. In fine weather, fishing and pleasure boats often cast anchor within the shelter of the headlands. Several markings and buoys guide boats inland.

20Km
5:30

There are strong winds, and it is recommended that you follow the footpath along the coast between the low dunes and the marshes wherever possible, to obtain at least a little shelter. As it runs along the 20 kilometres between Castel de la Mondrée and Barfleur, the GR223 crosses several roads running inland to small villages. The path passes a monument erected in memory of the shipwrecked submarine Le Prométhée, and comes to Joret fortress, which is in ruins. It then runs along beside the sea to the D26.

Detour, *45 mins*
Menhir de la Pierre Plantée

If you follow the D26 south, you will come to the area around Cosqueville, which has many druid monuments. A little later, after the intersection with the D216, you will find the 3 metres high Menhir de la Pierre Plantée on your left.

Head along the coast past the small fort. Turn right 300 metres later along the path leading to the Fontaine Saint-Benoit.

Fontaine Saint-Benoit
Pilgrims used to make their way to this spot, as its

You will then come to Pointe de Néville, where you can see a group of blockhouses. The path continues along beside the sea for another 2

waters were meant to possess healing powers. The cave was built from the remains of an old 12th century priory.

kilometres and meanders between Etang de Gattemare (lake) and the sea. You can see where the tide has flooded a series of old quarries on your right. You will then come to Havre de Roubary.

Havre de Roubary

This little port was a hive of activity at the beginning of this century, when the nearby sand and stone quarries were being mined to build the port of Le Havre.

You follow the coastline running east of Pointe de Barfleur.

Phare de Gatteville

This stone column 71 metres high was built between 1829 and 1835. It stands out on the Val de Saire coastline and warns sailors that they are approaching the reefs of Barfleur. Its light can be seen all the way to the banks of the Calvados.

You will pass close by to Phare de Gatteville (lighthouse).

In 1120, the rocks offshore caused the shipwreck of La Blanche-Nef (the White Ship) which was carrying the only son of Henri I, Duke of Normandy and King of England, and brought the Norman dynasty in England to an end.

The path crosses marshy land and joins up with the D116 at Crabec mill. This dates from the 15th century but is now used as a landmark by sailors. Take the coastal path left which leads to Barfleur.

BARFLEUR

🏠 🛆 ✕ ⚓ 🚌 ℹ

This is a picturesque fishing port with its shale-covered houses. The port has been very active since the arrival of the Normans in the 9th century. It has historic links with the Norman Conquest: the Mora, *the drakkar on which William, Duke of Normandy set sail in 1066 to England, was built here. A bronze plaque at the harbour entrance commemorates this departure.*

The GR223 around Cotentin ends here. However, there is a walk around the Val de Saire which enables you to complete a loop ending up at Tourlaville. (It is marked in white and red.)

INDEX

The many different kinds of accommodation in France are explained in the introduction. Here we include a selection of hotels and other addresses, which is by no means exhaustive — the hotels listed are usually in the one-star of two-star categories. We have given full postal addresses so bookings can be made.

There has been an explosive growth in bed and breakfast facilities (chambres d'hôte) in the past few years, and staying in these private homes can be especially interesting and rewarding. Local shops and the town hall (mairie) can usually direct you to one.

Details of bus/train connections have been provided wherever it was possible. We suggest you refer also to the map inside the front cover.

Ancteville 115
50200 Manche
⌂ *Gîte d'étape, M. Michel Esnouf, 'La Foulerie'*
☎ *33.45.27.64*
Anse du Brick 143
Anse des Moulinets 133
Arcouest (L') 16, 64
22620 Ploubazlanec
⌂ *Le Barbu* ☎ *96.55.86.98*
🚢 *Île de Bréhat*
Armor (L') 69
Auderville 135
Aumône (L') 21
Avranches 16, 101
50300 Manche
⌂ *Du Jardin des Plantes, 10 Place Carnot, M. Leroy*
☎ *33.58.03.68*
⌂ *Le Pratel, 24 Rue Vanniers*
☎ *33.68.35.41*
⌂ *Auberge St-Michel, 7 Place Gen-Patton*
☎ *33.58.01.91*
⌂ *Auberge de Jeunesse, 15 Rue du Jardin des Plantes*
☎ *33.58.06.54*
⌂ *Gîte d'étape, Ferme d'Apilly* ☎ *33.58.37.89*
🛈 *Office de Tourisme, Rue Gen.-de-Gaulle*
☎ *33.58.00.22*

Barfleur 15, 17, 147
50760 Manche
⌂ *Conquérant*
☎ *33.54.00.82*

🛈 *Quai H.-Chardar (July and August)*
Barnénez 97
Barneville-Carteret 17, 123
50270 Manche
⌂ *De Paris, M. Poitvin*
☎ *33.04.90.02*
⌂ *Les Isles, M. Masson*
☎ *33.04.90.76*
⌂ *L'Hermitage-Maison Duhamel* ☎ *33.04.96.29*
🛈 *Office de Tourisme, Rue des Écoles* ☎ *33.04.90.58*
🚌 *Portbail, Valegnes (in summer)*
Bas du Palais (Le) 23
Beg Léguer 83
Binic 16, 57
22520 Côtes-du-Nord
⌂ *Le Galion, 4 Avenue Foch M. Rispal* ☎ *96.73.61.30*
Biville 131
50440 Manche
⌂ *Gîte d'étape, M. Abbe Leloy, 'Presbytere'*
☎ *33.52.74.81*
Bonne Vierge Simolet 141
Bréhec 61
Bretteville-sur-Ay 119
Buguélès 73

Cabane Vauban 105
Cancale 15, 29
35260 Ille-et-Vilaine
⌂ *De la Pointe du Grouin, M. Simon* ☎ *99.89.60.55*
⌂ *Emeraude, 7. Quai*

Thomas, M. Chouamier-Grossin
☎ *99.89.61.76*
⌂ *Le Continental, sur le Port, M. Chouamier* ☎ *99.89.60.16*
🚌 *Saint-Malo, Dol, Pointe de Grouin*
Cap Fréhel 43
Carolles 17, 105
Carteret 123
Caserne (La) 19
⌂ *8 beds available in a bungalow for ramblers. M. Simon at the la Caserne campsite.*
🚌 *Pontorson, Mont-Saint-Michel*
Castel de la Mondrée 143
Chapelle du Verger 31
Châtellier (La) 27
Cherbourg 15, 17, 139
50100 Manche
⌂ *Louvre, 2 Rue H.-Dunant*
☎ *33.53.02.28*
⌂ *Angleterre, 8 Rue P. Tallnan* ☎ *33.53.70.06*
⌂ *Beauséjour, 26 Rue Grande Vallée* ☎ *33.53.10.30*
⌂ *Auberge de Jeunesse, 109 Avenue de Paris*
☎ *33.44.26.31*
🛈 *Office de Tourisme, 2 Quai Aléxandre-III* ☎ *33.43.52.02*
🚌 *Quercqueville, Tourlaville*
🚢 *Weymouth, Portsmouth (5–6 hours) Sealink UK Ltd*
☎ *(01) 834 8122*
🚢 *Portsmouth (5–6 hours) P&O European Ferries Ltd, UK*

☎ (0304) 203388
⛴ Poole (5 hours) Brittany Ferries, UK ☎ (0705) 827701
⛴ Cork, Irish Continental Line
Cherrueix 21
35120 Dol-de-Bretagne
(H) Parcs, Place Église
☎ 99.48.82.86
⌂ Gîte 1 km south at l'Aumône, M. Maillard
Cotentin (La) 47
Coudeville-Plage 109
Coutances 17, 113
50200 Manche
(H) Cositel, Route de Coutainville, M. Holley
☎ 33.07.51.64
(H) Grand Hotel, Place de la Gare, M. Turpin
☎ 33.45.06.55
(H) Relais du Viaduc, 25 Avenue de Verdun, M. Hossin
☎ 33.45.02.68
⌂ Gîte d'étape, M. Yves Lamy, 75v Rue d'Ilkley
☎ 33.45.10.92
🆔 Office de Tourisme, Rue Quesnel-Moriniere
☎ 33.45.17.79
Crec'h Goueno 73
Coz Port-Trégastel 79

Dahouët 47
Denneville-Plage 121
Diélette 129
Dinard 16, 35
35800 Ille-et-Vilaine
(H) Altair, 18 Bd. Féart, Mme Lemenager ☎ 99.46.13.58
(H) La Plage, 3 Bd. Féart, M. Sueur ☎ 99.46.14.87
(H) Host. Le Petit Robinson, on the D114 ☎ 99.46.14.82
⛴ Boat trips in summer to Saint-Malo
🚌 Paris
🚆 Rennes, Saint-Malo, Saint-Brieuc
Dol-de-Bretagne 16, 25
35120 Ille-et-Vilaine
(H) De Bretagne, 17 Pl. Chateaubriand, M. Haelling-Morel ☎ 99.48.02.03
(H) Logis de la Bresche Arthur, 36 Bd. Deminiac, M. Faveau ☎ 99.48.01.44
🆔 Office de Tourisme, 3 Grande Rue des Stuarts
☎ 99.48.15.37 🚆 Rennes, Pontorson, Saint-Malo, Dinan
Dourduff-en-Mer (Le) 99
Dragey 103
Dune (La) 103

Erquy 16, 45
22430 Côtes-du-Nord
(H) Beauséjour, Rue de la Corniche, M. Thebault
☎ 96.72.30.39
(H) Brigantin, Square Hôtel de Ville ☎ 96.72.32.14
(H) L'Escurial, Bd. Mer
☎ 96.72.31.56
🆔 Office de Tourisme, Bd. Mer ☎96.72.30.12
🚆 Saint-Brieuc, Pléherel
Étables-sur-Mer 16, 58

Far West (Le) 117
Flamanville 17, 127
Fond de la Baie 89
Fontaine-Saint-Benoit 145
Fort la Latte 43

Gare (La) 105
Gefosses 115
Genêts 103
50530 Sartilly (Manche)
⌂ Auberge de Jeunesse, Ancienne gare ☎ 33.70.82.63
Godelins (Les) 58
Goury 135
Granville 17, 107
50400 Manche
(H) 19 Rue G.-Clemenceau
☎ 33.50.17.31
(H) Michelet, 5 Rue J.-Michelet ☎ 33.50.06.55
(H) Le Phare, 11 Rue Port
☎ 33.50.12.94
🆔 Office de Tourisme, 15 Rue G.-Clemenceau
☎ 33.50.02.67
Grouin du Sud 103
Guerzit (Plage de) 95
Guesclin (Plage de) 31
Guildo (Le) 39
Guimaëc 91
Guimorais (La) 33

Havre de Roubary 147
Hatainville 125
Hauteville-sur-Mer 111
Hillion 49
Hirel 21, 27

Ile Grande 80
Ile Renote 79

Jospinet 47

Kérameau 87
Kérénoc 79

Kerguntuil 79
Kérity 63
Kerjolis 61
Kermagen 69

Lancieux 37
22770 Côtes-du-Nord
(H) Mer, Rue Plage
☎ 96.86.22.07
🚆 Dinard
Landemer 137
Lanloup 61
22580 Plouha
⌂ Hébergement, M. Boulbennec, Manoir de Kerjolis
☎ 99.22.33.47
Lannion 16, 127
22300 Côtes-du-Nord
(H) Porte de France, 5 Rue J.-Savidan ☎ 96.46.54.81
(H) Bretagne, 32 Avenue Gén. de Gaulle
☎ 96.37.00.33
⌂ Auberge de Jeunesse, 6 Rue du 73 Territorial
☎ 96.37.91.28
Lanros 67
Launay 87
Lessay 119
🚆 Coutances, Cherbourg
Lézardrieux 66
22740 Côtes-du-Nord
(H) Pont ☎ 96.20.10.59
Lézingar 91
Locquémeau 85
Locquirec 16, 90
29241 Finistère
(H) Rennenez
☎ 98.67.42.21
Loguivy-de-la-Mer 65
Loguivy-lès-Lannion 83
Louannec 75
Luzuret 69

Martin-Plage 55
Moitiers d'Allonne (Les) 125
Mont-Dol 25
Monthuchon 113
Montmartin-sur-Mer 111
50590 Manche
(H) Host. du Bon Vieux Temps
☎ 33.47.54.44
Mont-Saint-Michel (Le) 15, 17, 19
50116 Manche
(H) Du Guesclin, M. Nicolle
☎ 33.60.14.10
(H) De la Digue, Mme. Luizard-Bourdon
☎ 33.60.14.02
(H) K. Motel, M. Francois Fournier ☎ 33.60.14.18

🛈 Office de Tourisme, Corps
de Garde des Bourgeois
☎ 33.60.14.30
⚓
▬
Morieux 49
Morlaix 15, 16, 99
29210 Finistère
🏠 Europe, 1 Rue Aiguillon
☎ 98.62.11.99
🛈 Place Otages
☎ 98.62.14.94
⚓ Paris, Brest, Roscoff
Motte (La) 43
83920 Var
🏠 Les Pignatelles, Route
Bagnols ☎ 94.70.25.70
🏠 Auberge Fleurie
☎ 94.70.27.68
◻ Auberge de Jeunesse at
Kérivet (summer only)
Moulin de la Rive 91
Muneville-le-Bingard 115

Nanthouar 75
22660 Trélévern
◻ Gîte d'étape, Mme. Paul
Kremer Stella Maris
☎96.23.15.62
Nez de Voidries 135

Omonville-la-Rogue 135
50440 Beaumont-Hague,
Manche
🏠 Port ☎ 33.52.74.13

Paimpol 16, 63
22500 Côtes-du-Nord
🏠 Marne, 30 Rue Marne
☎ 96.20.82.16
🏠 Goelo, au Port
☎ 96.20.82.74
🏠 Chalutiers, 5 Quai Morand
☎ 96.20.82.15
◻ Auberge de Jeunesse,
Châteay de Keraoult
☎ 96.20.83.60
Palud de Kerarmel 97
Palus (Le) 59
Penvern 80
Perros-Guirec 16, 76
22700 Côtes-du-Nord
🏠 Printania, 12 Rue
Bons-Enfants ☎ 96.23.21.00
🏠 France, 14 Rue Rouzig
☎ 96.23.20.27
🏠 Morgane, 46 Avenue
Casino ☎ 96.23.22.80
🛈 Office de Tourisme, 21
Place Hôtel de Ville
☎ 96.23.21.15
Pieux (Les) 127

Pirou-le-Pont 17, 115
Plage Bonaparte 60
Plage de Bretteville-sur-Ay,
see Bretteville-sur-Ay
Plage de Edenville 105
Plage du Guerzit,
see Guerzit
Plage de Guesclin,
see Guesclin
Planguenoual 47
Pléherel-Plage 43
▬ Saint-Brieuc
Pléneuf-Val-André 47
22370 Côtes-du-Nord
🏠 Grand Hotel du Val Andre,
Rue Amiral-Charner
☎ 96.72.20.56
🏠 Clemenceau, 131 Rue
Clemenceau ☎ 96.72.23.70
🏠 Casino, 10 Rue Ch. Cotard
☎ 96.72.20.22
🏠 Ajoncs d'Or, Plage des
Vallées ☎ 96.72.29.81
Plérin 53
Plestin-les-Grèves 89
Pleubian 69
Ploubazlanec 63
Plouezoc'h 97
Plougasnou 93
29228 Finistère
🏠 France, Place Église
☎ 98.67.30.15
🛈 Rue des Martyrs
☎ 98.67.31.88
Plougrescant 73
22820
◻ Gîte d'étape, Crec'h
Gweno ☎ 96.92.54.55
Plouha 59
Ploujean 99
Ploumanac'h 16, 77
22700 Perros-Guirec
🏠 Parc ☎ 96.23.24.88
🏠 Phare ☎ 96.23.23.08
Pointe de Annalouesten 95
Pointe de Champ du Port 45
Pointe de Château-Richeux
27
Pointe du Corbeau (La) 90
Pointe de Grouin 16, 29
35260 Cancale
🏠 Pointe du Grouin
☎ 99.89.60.55
▬ Cancale
Pointe de Primel (La) 94
Pointe de Roselier 55
Pont (Le) 35
Pont de Beauvoir 19
Pont de la Roque (Le) 111
Pont-Rolland (Le) 49
Pordic 57
Portbail 17, 21
50580 Manche
🏠 La Galiche, M. Genest
☎ 33.04.84.18

▬ Cherbourg; Carentin and
Valognes (in summer)
⚓ Guernsey, Jersey
Port-Blanc 75
22710 Penvenan
Côtes-du-Nord
🏠 Iles ☎ 96.92.66.49
🏠 Le Rocher
☎ 96.92.64.97
🏠 Grand Hôtel, Bd. de la
Mer, M. Monfrance
☎ 96.92.66.52
Port du Diben 95
Port-à-la-Duc 41
Port Lazo 63
Port L'Epine 75
Port-Morvan (Le) 47
Port Racine, see
St-Germain des Vaux
Port-au-Sud-Est 43
Portrieux,
see Saint-Quay-Portrieux
Porz Even 63
Porz-Hir 73
Poul Rodou (Plage de) 91

Quatre Salines (Les) 21
Québo (Le) 69
Quercqueville 139

Roche (La) 135
Roche-Jaune (La) 71
Rosaires (Les) 56
Roscoff 15
29211 Finistère
🏠 Talabardon, Place Église
☎ 98.61.24.95
🏠 Bellevue, Rue Jeanne
d'Arc ☎ 98.61.23.38
🏠 Les Tamaris, Rue Edouard
Corbiere ☎ 98.61.22.99
🛈 Rue Gambetta
☎ 98.69.70.70
⚓ Morlaix
⚓ Plymouth (6–7 hours)
Brittany Ferries, UK
☎ (0705) 827701
Rothéneuf 33
▬ Saint-Malo
Roz-sur-Couesnon 23
Rozel (Le) 17, 127
Roz-Ven 31

Sables-d'Or-les-Pins 45
22240 Fréhel, Côtes-du-Nord
🏠 Au Bon Accueil, M.
Rolland ☎ 96.41.42.19
🏠 De Diane, M. Rabardel
☎ 96.41.42.07
🏠 L'Abordage, Bd. de la
Mer, M. Mace
☎ 96.41.51.11

▬ *Saint-Brieuc, Pléherel*
Saint-Benoît-des-Ondes 27
Saint-Briac 16, 37
▬ *Dinard, Lancieux*
Saint-Brieuc 16, 51
22000 Côtes-du-Nord
🏠 *Le Griffon, Rue de*
Guernesey ☎ *96.94.57.62*
🏠 *Pomme d'Or, Avenue*
Langueux ☎ *96.61.12.10*
🏠 *St-Georges, 1 ter Rue de*
Robien ☎ *96.94.24.06*
🛈 *Office de Tourisme, 7 Rue*
St.-Goueno ☎ *96.33.32.50*
▬
▬ *Saint-Quay-Portrieux,*
Paimpol, Saint-Laurent, Les
Rosaires
Saint Broladre 23
Saint-Cast-le-Guildo 16, 41
22380 Côtes-du-Nord
🏠 *Ar Vro, Grande Plage*
☎ *96.41.85.01*
🏠 *Dunes, Rue Primauguet*
☎ *96.41.80.31*
🏠 *Arcades, Rue Piétonne*
☎ *96.41.80.50*
🛈 *Office de Tourisme, Place*
Gen.de-Gaulle
☎ *96.41.81.52*
▬ *Lamballe (summer)*
Saint-Efflam 89
Saint-Germain-sur-Ay 119
Saint-Germain des Vaux 135
50440 Beaumont-Hague
Manche
🏠 *L'Erguillère, A Port Racine*
☎ *33.52.75.31*
Saint-Jacut-de-la-Mer 16, 39
22750 Côtes-du-Nord
🏠 *Vieux Moulin*
☎ *96.27.71.02*
▬ *Dinan*
Saint-Jean-du-Doigt 92
Saint-Jean-le-Thomas 105
50530 Sartilly Manche
🏠 *Des Bains, M. Gautier*
☎ *33.48.84.20*
Saint Léonard 103
Saint-Lunaire 16, 37
Saint-Malo 15, 16, 35
35400 Ille-et-Vilaine

🏠 *Armor, 8 Rue R. Schuman,*
M. Colleu ☎ *99.56.00.75*
🏠 *De la Pomme d'Argent,*
24 Bd. des Talards, M. Coquelin
☎ *99.56.12.39*
🏠 *De la Porte Sainte Pierre, 2*
Place du Guest, Mme.
Bertonniere ☎ *99.40.91.27*
🏠 *Grand Hotel de*
Courtoisville, 69 Bd. Herbert,
M. Detrois ☎ *99.40.83.83*
🛈 *Office de Tourisme,*
Esplanade St-Vincent
☎ *99.56.64.48*
▬ *Dol, Rennes, Pontorson*
▬ *Cancale, Pontorson,*
Fougères, Rennes, Dinan
⚓ *Portsmouth (9–10 hours)*
Brittany Ferries, UK
☎ *(0705) 827701*
⚓ *Jersey (1½–2½ hours)*
Commodore Shipping Services
☎ *(0534 71263) and*
Emeraude Ferries
☎ *(0534 74458)*
⚓ *Guernsey (2½ hours,*
passengers only) Condor
Hydrofoil ☎ *(0481) 26121*
⚓ *Boat trips to Dinard in*
season
Saint-Marc 59
Saint-Marcan 23
⌂ *Gîte. Mme. Clémont at*
the town hall
▬ *From Colombel on D797*
to Pontorson, Saint-Malo
Saint-Michel-en-Grève 87
22300 Lannion
🏠 *Plage* ☎ *96.35.74.43*
Saint-Pair-sur-Mer 107
Saint-Quay-Portrieux 16, 59
22410 Côtes-du-Nord
🏠 *Le Bretagne, M. Cassin*
☎ *96.70.40.91*
🏠 *Le Gerbot d'Avoine, M.*
Lucas ☎ *96.79.40.09*
🛈 *Office de Tourisme, 17 bis*
Rue Jeanne-d'Arc
☎ *96.70.40.64*
Saint-Riom 63
Saint-Samson 195
Sciotot 127

Siouville 129
Surtainville 125
Surville 119

Térénez 95
Toëno (Le) 81
22560 Trébeurden
⌂ *Auberge de Jeunesse,*
Pors Toëno
☎ *96.23.52.22*
Toul an Héry 89
Tourlaville 141
▬ *Cherbourg*
Tournemine 57
Trébeurden 16, 83
Tréguier 16, 71
22220 Côtes-du-Nord
🏠 *Kastell Dinec'h, Route de*
Lannion ☎ *96.92.49.39*
🏠 *Estuaire, Place Gén-de-*
Gaulle ☎ *96.92.30.25*
Trestel 75
Tréveneuc 59
Ty Guen 67
22610 Pleubian
⌂ *Gîte d'étape, Milan ar*
Goas, Association Communes
☎ *96.22.90.68*

Urville-Nacqueville 139
50460 Querqueville
🏠 *Beaurivate*
☎ *33.03.52.40*
▬ *Cherbourg*

Val (Le) 16, 49
Ville-Hardrieux (La) 43
Vauville 133
Ville-ès-Offrans (La) 33
Vivier-sur-Mer (Le) 21
35960 Ille-et-Vilaine
🏠 *De Bretagne, Mm. Bunoult*
☎ *99.48.91.74*

Yaudet (Le) 85
Yffiniac 51